John Donne's Poetry

John Donne's Poetry

WILBUR SANDERS

*Fellow of Selwyn College and
Lecturer in English in the University of Cambridge*

Cambridge University Press

Published by the Syndics of the Cambridge University Press
Bentley House, 200 Euston Road, London NW1 2DB
American Branch: 32 East 57th Street, New York, N.Y.10022

© Cambridge University Press 1971

Library of Congress Catalogue Card Number: 75–149436

ISBNS:
0 521 07968 3 hard covers
0 521 09909 9 paperback

First published in 1971
First paperback edition 1974

First printed in Great Britain
by W & J Mackay & Co Ltd, Chatham
Reprinted in Great Britain by
Redwood Burn Limited, Trowbridge & Esher

Contents

A note on texts

Grierson's Oxford Standard Authors edition of 1933 still offers the most viable and most readily available text; and, unless otherwise stated, the text given will be his. What deviations there are usually derive from Helen Gardner's editions of *The Divine Poems* (Oxford, 1952) and *The Elegies and the Songs and Sonnets* (Oxford, 1965). Once or twice I have adopted a manuscript reading which both these editors have rejected. Reasons for these divergences are given in a footnote. The Sermons are quoted from the ten-volume University of California Press edition, ed. G. R. Potter and Evelyn M. Simpson, and I have used the text of the *Paradoxes* given in Evelyn Simpson's *John Donne: Selected Prose* (Oxford, 1967), which, though not complete, has at least been edited.

...it will be further found, that when Authors shall have at length raised themselves into general admiration and maintained their ground, errors and prejudices have prevailed concerning their genius and their works, which the few who are conscious of those errors and prejudices would deplore; if they were not recompensed by perceiving that there are select Spirits for whom it is ordained that their fame shall be in the world an existence like that of Virtue, which owes its being to the struggles it makes, and its vigour to the enemies whom it provokes; – a vivacious quality, ever doomed to meet with opposition, and still triumphing over it...

WORDSWORTH, 'Essay Supplementary', 1815

'Combinations of confused magnificence'
Donne and Dr Johnson

It often comes about that when a writer is conceded classic status he stops being read – at least in any important sense of the verb 'to read'. It happened to Milton. It happened to Wordsworth. It has, in a sense, happened to Lawrence who, though he proved intractable to assimilation by doctoral thesis, remained nevertheless so unhappily accessible to an undisciplined reading that notions of his importance tend now to derive their currency rather from vulgarising film-scripts than from what he wrote. It's the price a writer pays, I suppose, for addressing his contemporaries with that commanding degree of relevance. But the results of this peculiar combination of *pro forma* adulation and practical neglect can be seen in eighteenth-century Miltonising, in Victorian sub-Wordsworthianism, and in all the unconscious proto-Chatterleyism of the modern popular novel.

In Donne's case, the first wave of slack adulation gave us the decadent phase of metaphysical poetry; and the second wave has left us with a Donne whom every schoolboy knows is a great poet, whom many students of English Literature suspect is not, but of whose classic status, anyway, we possess no cogent contemporary account.

Not that interesting things haven't been written about Donne (my debts to them, conscious and unconscious, will be plain in what follows), nor that we haven't had some classic – and classically cryptic – criticism of him: notably from Coleridge, Eliot and Leavis. But the state of affairs upon which Eliot reported in 1921 – 'It would be a fruitful work, and one requiring a substantial book, to break up the classification of Johnson (for there has been none since)[1] – remains fundamentally unchanged. Eliot's own redefinition, in that essay, of the class, 'metaphysical poetry', in terms of 'a mechanism of

1 'The Metaphysical Poets', *Selected Essays* (1951), p. 291.

sensibility which could devour any kind of experience', was not in itself that fruitful work which could 'break up' the Johnsonian classification (however generally it may have supplanted it in the manuals of literary history), because at the end of the undertaking we are still left conceiving the essential metaphysicalness of the metaphysicals as a function of their *peculiarity*. The poetic faculty which 'amalgamates disparate experience', and fuses Spinoza with the smell of cooking, is proffered as the factor by which the metaphysical sensibility is marked off from 'the ordinary man's experience'. So that Johnson's case about the gratuitous oddity of the poetry is effectively conceded, while the illusion that it is being rebutted is sustained by a skilful transformation of the oddity into something more modern, and hence less recognisable as gratuitous. But the just comment upon a 'new whole' composed variously of a philosopher and a typewriter, cooking-smells and a love affair (if it wasn't merely Eliot free-associating at *his* typewriter) is surely Johnson's: 'heterogeneous ideas yoked by violence together'. As an account of something one is proposing to call 'unification of sensibility', it is trivialising.

A great deal of the difficulty here stems from the determination (which Eliot inherited from Johnson) to talk about so vast a variety of poetic experiences as if they were all of a kind, explicable in terms of a single 'mechanism'. Like so many of the liberators, Eliot fell under the spell of the classification he came to break up. But that 'spell' itself is a fact of literary history that cries out for comment.

For it was not just Eliot who allowed Johnson to impose upon him a grouping of seventeenth-century poets which has the immediate critical consequence of locating in Donne an embryonic Cleveland (and once the grouping is admitted Donne must fall under some, at least, of Johnson's strictures): it was the general reading public. And if we have assented to the classification, could it not be because an impartial reading of Donne simply does communicate the conviction that the embryo is there? Perhaps Johnson has been incomparably the most influential critic Donne ever had, precisely because he laid his finger on a critical raw-spot that most readers smart under. This is so manifest a truth that I shouldn't have the banality to propose it, if it weren't that it is a truth Donne's admirers seem never to have taken seriously. Their reaction is normally a testy concession – 'Oh well, yes. Of course!' (implying that, though true, it doesn't matter) –

followed by a thunderous 'But'. Nor, oddly enough, have Donne's detractors seen how Johnson struck at the root of the matter. Unless one counts such vivacious crankinesses as C. S. Lewis's cocking-of-a-snook at fashionable orthodoxy[1] – an operation as deeply conventional as the Donne-worship it was pleased to deride – the critical question has on neither side been pursued with the pertinacity it ought to have exacted. And as a result, the greatness of Donne, in so far as it is admitted – and how long, in this state of things, can it go on being admitted? – is more often something under which readers bow, than something in which they rejoice. One must except (as so often) Dr Leavis, who plainly is rejoicing in his Donne;[2] but in his mind the doubt either never gained lodgement, or it has been long since laid to rest; and the great poet he offers us, consequently, the poet who compels by a kind of 'irresistible rightness' (and that is certainly the way the case must be made), is equally present in the *Satyres* and the *Songs and Sonets*. That is not very consoling to the reader who experiences some difficulty in locating the rightness, and doesn't, when he has, find it always irresistible.

I think the case of Eliot is both more representative and depressing. For of course, there was a second essay on Donne, ominously entitled 'Donne in our Time'. It's surely noteworthy that the man who had, as it were, in 1921, given Donne in marriage to the reading public (albeit with Chapman concealed among the baggage), should, in 1931, have been faithless enough to jeer at the public for the alacrity with which it had accepted his gift:

In Donne, there is a manifest fissure between thought and sensibility, a chasm which in his poetry he bridged in his own way, which was not the way of medieval poetry. His learning is just information suffused with emotion, or combined with emotion not essentially relevant to it.[3]

The heartless thoroughness with which he casts off his misbegotten child is a striking critical portent. And however little one may warm to the tone of the recantation, or to its implied intellectual ambience – an ambience which permits him the smug certainty that Donne's

---

1 'Donne and Love Poetry in the Seventeenth Century', *Seventeenth-Century Studies presented to Sir Herbert Grierson* (1938).
2 'The Line of Wit', *Revaluation* (1936); 'Imagery and Movement', *Scrutiny*, XIII (1945), 119 f.
3 T. Spencer (ed.), *A Garland for John Donne* (1931), p. 8.

'cast of mind was such as made it impossible to be a constructive philosopher or a mystic' (those two well-known and generally accessible states of being), and one which encourages the critic to indulge an urbane suspicion that, if Donne was a rake, then he was a very conventional rake – it is unmistakably a conscientious demolition of all his old bridgeheads.

The passage goes on,

But perhaps one reason why Donne has appealed so powerfully to the recent time is that there is in his poetry hardly any attempt at organisation; rather a puzzled and humorous shuffling of the pieces; and we are inclined to read our own more conscious awareness of the apparent irrelevance and unrelatedness of things into the mind of Donne.

If this is indeed the 'inclination' in Eliot which had been satisfying itself upon Donne, he did well to deny it to himself. The advocacy Donne could have expected to win from such a source could only have had the effect of discrediting him. But equally, if there is some other, better case to be made, it will have to be made without trusting too implicitly to such uncertain allies as Eliot himself.

For there was something, surely, about the original account which lent itself to this lordly subversion. To say that a poet feels his thought as immediately as the odour of a rose, though it has the air of being rather complimentary, is to put the matter sufficiently aesthetically to facilitate the subsequent debasement, and the logical sleight that goes with it:

he was more interested in *ideas* themselves as objects than in the *truth* of ideas;

and so, by a precipitate transition, we arrive at a Donne given to 'petting and teasing' his 'mental objects', a poet whose distinction, such as it is, resides primarily in *trouvailles*, 'odd and beautiful objects' dredged up from the bottom of the Ocean of the Mind. (We now see how 'feeling one's thought as the odour of a rose' might be the wrong way to feel it, and what a disabling potential lay concealed in Eliot's interest in 'bracelets of bright hair about the bone' as the type of 'Donne's most successful and characteristic effects'.) 'Thought', in the sense he finishes by attributing it to Donne, is at best a matter of curiosity – that was the critical weight of those striking comparisons with Laforgue.

I don't want to suggest that we see, in this diagnosis, merely a characteristic Eliot perversity – though it is that. Nor am I forgetting that the short answer to all the 1931 insinuations had been given in the 1921 essay: 'A philosophical theory *which has entered into poetry* is established, for its truth or falsity in one sense ceases to matter, and its truth in another sense is proved' – an affirmation the full embracing of which would have rendered impossible those specious appeals to 'orthodoxy' with which Eliot buttresses the argument of the later essay. But the 'recantation' carries enough conviction to intimate that it was, in some sense, what he meant to say; and the suspect quality in Donne it fastens upon is, significantly, the same that moved Johnson to protest: a sense that, for this kind of 'wit', the ideas are more important than their truth.

The question about the 'truth' of Donne's poetry is plainly a central one, and not to be side-stepped. Johnson's case for the prosecution, though it is refuted with monotonous and stupefying regularity on every campus in the Western world, still commands an attention and respect which the refutations have never secured for themselves. The question remains open, for all the tranquillising labours of the critics. And that is as it should be: if it were ever 'closed', the volumes of Donne's poetry would be closed too – for the last time.

What I'm proposing, however, is beginning to sound like some fierce and remorseless conditioning of the intellectual muscles, commando-training for the assault upon Donne. There is one spectacular leap over all these thorny obstacles which we might therefore ponder, since it forms, I'm sure, a part of any generous response to the richness of Donne's poetry. It is the leap taken by that quintessentially generous reader, Coleridge, as he enthusiastically annotates his copy of Donne:

This power of dissolving orient pearls, worth a kingdom, in a health to a whore! – this absolute right of dominion over all thoughts, that dukes are bid to clean his shoes, and are yet honoured by it!...this lordliness of opulence!... Wonder-exciting vigour, intenseness and peculiarity of thought, using at will the almost boundless stores of a capacious memory, and exercised on subjects, where we have no right to expect it – this is the wit of Donne![1]

What, viewed from one angle, is an irresponsibility of imagination, is from another an opulence of feeling. And what nettled Johnson as a

[1] R. F. Brinkley (ed.), *Coleridge on the Seventeenth Century* (1955), pp. 522 and 526.

singularity, a *peculiarity* of mind, may be just as intensely felt as bound-less fertility – though to feel it as that, is to discern a peculiarity creatively transformed, purged of all in it that is merely singular and idiosyncratic.

'Intenseness and peculiarity of thought' is, I suppose, the same quality that Johnson referred to as 'combinations of confused magni-ficence', but it has been suffused with the warmth of a responsive and ardent mind. The difference between Coleridge and Johnson, as readers, is that Coleridge is prepared to meet the poetry with the spirited resistance Donne's outrageousness perpetually invites (thus making it not only tolerable, but 'wonder-exciting'); whereas John-son is chiefly impressed by the preposterousness of Donne's ever ex-pecting that of him. Coleridge, as we shall see, had his own wry reservations to register about Donne; but they did not, finally, ob-struct the free flow of his admiration. That is the model of ardent im-partiality that I want to keep in view throughout the following pages.

One can only responsibly address oneself to Johnson's challenge in Johnson's spirit – though it is equally the spirit of Coleridge's criticism:

I rejoice to concur with the common reader; for by the common sense of readers uncorrupted with literary prejudices, after all the refinements of subtility and the dogmatism of learning, must be decided all claim to poetical honours.[1]

Every reading, if it is at all a lively one, is a fresh, though not neces-sarily a first, reading; and its freshness is enjoyably experienced as a part of some larger human concurrence. If, as it begins to appear, Donne's reputation, however fortified with 'subtilty' and 'learning', does *not* reflect 'the common sense of readers', his greatness will have to be winnowed out from the mere reputation before it can be fully possessed.

Greatness in art – to rehearse some necessary truisms – is something personally felt, or it is nothing. Felt first of all, perhaps, as a fulness: 'that comprehension and expanse of thought which at once fills the whole mind, and of which the first effect is sudden astonishment, and the second rational admiration'. (That is Dr Johnson on 'the sublime',[2]

---

[1] *Life of Gray.*

[2] *Life of Cowley.* (Unless otherwise indicated, all subsequent references to Johnson are to the dozen or so pages of that *Life* where he discusses the 'metaphysical poets'.)

a quality he found it necessary to define – and the irony is a reminder of our critical predicament here – because he detected in Donne a notable lack of it.) To receive that fulness as doctrine, is not to receive it at all; because then, instead of there being the 'exertion of a co-operating power in the mind of the reader',[1] which Wordsworth saw as an essential part of the poetic process, the mind of the reader sinks in inert lethargy under the dead weight of reputation. Literature becomes a mental idol. The 'co-operating power' atrophies. We cease to weigh what we read against the fullest sense of life we can command, and we come to lack, as a result, the mental space or the human amplitude within which we might grasp the greatness.

But greatness has its more public dimension too; because, as Wordsworth goes on to observe, 'Of genius, in the fine arts, the only infallible sign is the widening the sphere of human sensibility, for the delight, honour, and benefit of human nature.' Which is not to say that one seeks out genius in order to be delighted, honoured and benefited: the effect of the kind of spaciousness Wordsworth has in mind is pretty much to dispel such self-absorbed motivation. In the presence of greatness one frets far less about one's personal relation to the greatness, than one finds an impersonal satisfaction in the fact that it exists; and it is one of the prerogatives of greatness to have just this effect. But the being aware of its existence exacts something further. We hail a writer as a classic precisely because of his capacity to incite to the finest kind of consciousness: his very excellence is what animates and empowers the critical scrutiny of it. And as the mind finds increasing satisfaction in that task, as the conviction of the excellence grows, so the author's capacity to sustain the scrutiny becomes a source of multiplying pleasure – criticism and appreciation become a single complex act.

This cumulative satisfaction, which simultaneously refines and enlarges our sense of the writer's stature, is what ensures that we shall go on asking, not nigglingly and waspishly, but warmly and soberly, *why* he is a classic, and perhaps even more importantly, *where* he is a classic. Go on asking, how does Donne widen the sphere of human sensibility? What does he offer for the delight, honour and benefit of human nature? Where is the human truth to be most intensely encountered? Why great? Wherefore classic?

[1] 'Essay, Supplementary to the Preface' (1815).

7

There is a danger, however, that in putting these questions too baldly to the poetry one merely elicits from it confirmation of the doctrine of human nature one already, and on other grounds, espouses. And that activity, whatever general uses it may serve, is not to be confused with the activity of reading Donne. We want a foothold upon some solid human ground, but one which can also be specified in concrete observations upon the poetry Donne wrote. I think that foothold is to be found where Dr Leavis found it – in that extraordinary Donne *voice* which, in a collection of seventeenth-century verse, effortlessly transforms the kind of attention we are prompted to give it, so that (as Leavis has it) 'we read on as we read the living'. It's an obvious comment; most important comments are. But it isolates something about Donne which often commands respect long before one is reading with anything like full comprehension: I mean that quality of utterance which implies, indeed creates, a body of experience and a 'life' in a sense more important, perhaps, than the biographical. It is the *life* that one is attending to when, like a dominant presence in a room full of chatter, Donne detaches himself from the surrounding loquacity by an individual vibrancy and directness, so that one finds oneself listening with a spirited interest which is largely unconscious of the mechanisms of communication.

I start with the Donne 'voice', not with the Donne philosophy, or the Donne conceit, or the Donne poetic, or the Donne toughness, because all those qualities, and indeed the whole idiosyncrasy of 'the Donne manner', form the spearhead, as we've seen, of the critical assault upon him. The voice is not so easily dismissed:

> Love is a growing, or full constant light;
> And his first minute, after noone, is night.
>
> ('A Lecture upon the Shadow')

It might be, at first sight, the voice of the pundit, the self-appointed sage. But the generalising weight on the word 'love', the grave pausing upon it, feels neither gratuitous nor arbitrary. There seems a weight of implicit experience behind it. Only when the second line is complete and the metaphor of love-as-sun is suddenly shattered, do we discover what the experience is, as we are plunged into darkness ('...is *night*'). There's a world of grim compression in that single plain noun. Behind the pronouncement, in a sense validating it, lie more than one of these catastrophic blackouts.

8

Donne is offering – perilous undertaking – to define love. And I think we can feel more powerfully the weight and authority he gives his generalities if we put them beside Marvell's faintly quizzical 'Definition of Love'.

> My Love is of a birth as rare
> As 'tis for object strange and high:
> It was begotten by despair
> Upon Impossibility.

The verse has a queer, stiff-legged, bird-like gait; and there is something comparatively flimsy about tone and sentiment ('rare...strange ...high'). Where Donne takes his sun metaphor with such seriousness that he is prepared to break its back in the interests of veracity, Marvell almost plays with his personifications – especially with the conceit of the love's 'rare birth', in which the elegant appositeness of the figure is allowed to cloud the serious sense in which despair *at* the impossibility was the real engendering of the love. So that one glimpses the 'despair' only through superimposed layers of defensive irony. The perception is thwarted, one might put it this way, by a speaking voice which does not include among its range of tones Donne's kind of authority, and can only simulate it by means of wry self-depreciation. Where Donne possesses his love-experience and speaks from the centre of it, Marvell stands uneasily perched on its edge, poised for flight, or retraction, or self-mockery.

But Donne's authority is not operating to persuade us of the truth of abstract propositions. The pressure of experience felt in the voice doesn't have that kind of validating force. There is the same quality of weight about lines which very nearly contradict 'A Lecture upon a Shadow':

> Love, all alike, no season knowes, nor clyme,
> Nor houres, dayes, moneths, which are the rags of time.
> ('The Sunne Rising')

Lovers, of course, are always making this kind of exorbitant claim, and a very foolish one it looks on the face of it – especially in a poem about 'The Sunne Rising'. But for all the superficial resemblance it bears to a familiar romantic delusion of immortality in love, it is utterly unlike it at its core. Again, it is the vibrancy of the voice that arrests the ear,

9

a vibrancy here partly of contempt ('*rags* of time') but also of exulta-
tion. Even the low-keyed 'houres, dayes, moneths' (overtly they are
being dismissed from consideration) begin to resonate with that
exultancy. Implicit in the speech movement, and given body in the
voice, is a steady conviction that will not be imposed upon; one
which knows exactly the extent of its exorbitance and, even more
firmly, the reason for it: 'Tell me not about hours, days, months! I
know what I possess.'

If I say that this steadiness has a peculiarly masculine resonance
about it, I'm not just referring to fashionable critical cliché about 'the
manly Donne' (though this cliché is old enough to have acquired
some respectability – 'a line/Of masculine expression' was what
Carew saw, in 1633, as one of Donne's great contributions to English
poetry). I mean that the masculinity is one of the truly notable things
about the voice here. There are certain emotional 'styles' that are not
common to both sexes, and this swelling, almost boasting exultancy is
one of them. I can imagine the lines in the mouth of a woman only at
the cost of some stridency; and stridency, though it is the endemic
disease of all affirmation, is exactly what Donne avoids here. In its
place, vibrating with a low-keyed energy it can scarcely contain, we
get the note of sure male triumph – 'Love, all alike, no season knowes,
nor clyme...'

Masculine, though: not buckish. It's not the male defined in
opposition to, or in defiance of, the female. That would sound like this:

> Tell me not, sweet, I am unkind,
>   That from the nunnery
> Of thy chaste breast and quiet mind,
>   To war and arms I fly.
>
> True, a new mistress now I chase,
>   The first foe in the field;
> And with a stronger faith embrace
>   A sword, a horse, a shield.
>
> Yet this inconstancy is such
>   As you too shall adore...

That voice – Richard Lovelace's – speaks (with some complacency)
out of the exclusively male preserve, putting the woman straight on
some misconceptions that she is bound (being a woman – a creature

with a native incomprehension of 'war and arms') to fall into. The
female world, that sadly yet deliciously restrictive 'nunnery', can
offer, finally, only the weak attractions of chastity and quiet to the
aspiring male mind, which therefore 'flies' (revealing verb) to war
and arms. The casual enormity with which something very close to
insult is offered as compliment – equating the 'chase' of a mistress
with the chase of an enemy – and the incidental preference expressed
for 'embracing' his horse rather than his love – these are the sorts of
grossness that can be expected when the female world is seen merely
as enhancing and lending lustre to the male.

When Donne, in the Song 'Sweetest love, I do not goe', meets a
similar situation, the fineness of feeling and the delicacy of tone make
a striking contrast. The woman in Lovelace's poem is, at best,
addressed. Donne *speaks to* his woman, his eyes full on her face affec-
tionately reading her expression.

> Sweetest love, I do not goe,
>   For weariness of thee,
> Nor in hope the world can show
>   A fitter Love for mee;
>   But since that I
>   Must dye at last, 'tis best,
>   To use my selfe in jest
>   Thus by fain'd deaths to dye.

It is real speech to a real person – not simply because the poem is
implicitly taking account of the reproachful questions the woman has
asked ('Are you tired of me, then? Must I see you set out in search of
new conquests? Why do you, by going, force these suspicions upon
me?') – though the taking account of them, as questions requiring
something fuller in the way of an answer than the standard buckish
rationalisation, immediately distinguishes Donne's poem from Love-
lace's. But there is also the sense one gets that his voice has had to
develop a whole new expressive register to deal with his acute
consciousness of the woman's presence and her distress. In the shared
poignancy of that ineffectual joke about 'fain'd deaths', for instance,
the man's voice has modulated itself to take in a womanly tenderness
of fiction.

If one looks hard at those implicit reproaches, one sees what it is in
her that he is meeting: her questions all spring from a fear that the

impervious, insensitive male order ('war and arms') will supervene, a fear of being fobbed off with such impertinent insincerities as the one which ends the Lovelace poem:

> I could not love thee, dear, so much,
> Lov'd I not Honour more.

Donne's answer to her question is to show that such fears are groundless, that his maleness defines itself fully only in responding to her femaleness – taking her woman's fears into his own consciousness and giving them back to her clothed in his man's tenderness. That tonal sensitivity, the voice responding subtly and feelingly to the woman's presence, has a great deal to do with Donne's authority as a love-poet.

In the following lines from 'A Valediction: Of Weeping', the reality of the woman's feelings of grief progressively takes over the man's voice with their broken rhythms:

> O more then Moone,
> Draw not up seas to drowne me in thy sphaere,
> Weepe me not dead, in thine armes, but forbeare
> To teach the sea, what it may doe too soone...

Yet for all that astonishing responsiveness – moving from the wry-mournful adoration of the first line, through the long, yearning, pleading cadence of the second, until he is actually helplessly afloat on the seas of her grief, shaken physically by it – still the note of grim foreboding in the last line, the compressed realism of that 'too soone', are all the man's own, a return upon his male dignity which is as natural and as fitting as the woman's immersion in her grief was. The two together, in delicate interaction, do something substantial for the honour of human nature. We are given courtesy in an authentic and necessary manifestation – not least in the eloquent lyricism that contains so much passion within its purity of vocal line.

Because Donne is so unconstrainedly alive to the woman's reality, his celebration of her – when that is what he is moved to – has an utter grace of sentiment that has given us some of the most, in every sense, beautiful lines a love-poet ever wrote:

> Ev'ry thy haire for love to worke upon
> Is much too much, some fitter must be sought;
> For, nor in nothing, nor in things
> Extreme, and scatt'ring bright, can love inhere...
>
>   ('Aire and Angels')

There is no taint here of the possessiveness of passion: he gives her back, as it were, to the world which alone is vast enough to do justice to her magnificence – 'Ev'ry thy haire…Is much too much…' – with a joyously defeated, laughing despair over ever encompassing the riches he miraculously possesses. You might call it the supreme compliment of man to woman, if 'compliment' were not so inert a word for the keen edge of delight upon the lines. Yet it is nothing *less* than a mere record of a rapture: even at the heart of the ecstasy Donne retains his sense of proportion and decorum ('…some fitter must be sought'), and this paean of delight is itself part of an extended argument.

For the quality of 'authority' in Donne, as well as being a personal attribute, is also something we repeatedly see being won in the poems. This is more than a matter of his much-noted addiction to logical structures – as if these were things imposed upon the feeling. The delight (or the anguish) is what generates the *measure*, and the measure is to be felt everywhere: in the syntax, the intonation, the verse movement, the weighing of words (the way, for instance, the rapt improvisation of 'Extreme, and scatt'ring bright' gives place to the grave intellection of 'inhere'). Donne is never content with feeling which has been separated from understanding. Utterance is not for him a way of relieving his feelings: it is a way of discovering, creating, realising his feelings. Hence, contained within the immediate and exultant emotion of 'Aire and Angels', a measured quality – the voice of a man who knows the precise cost of his words.

At times, indeed, he knows it with anguish:

> O perverse sexe, where none is true but shee,
> Who's therefore true, because her truth kills mee.
> ('Twicknam Garden')

Words like 'true' and 'truth', in this context, are not promissory notes drawn on problematical emotions, but good ringing coin. It is precisely the question of *how* he knows 'truth' to be the right word for what she is that Donne is wrestling with here. 'Meaning's press and screw' (in a phrase Coleridge used of Donne) is twisted down fiercely upon the experience ('*therefore* true, *because*…') to extract the essence of his situation; and the strenuous process comes across to us in the set teeth and the grim pausing necessitated equally by sense, and by the consonantal clotting of sound ('because her truth kills mee'). Perhaps it was this kind of mental operation that Donne had in mind when he spoke to a friend of 'My verse, the strict Map of my misery' (Verse Letter 'To Mr T.W.').

The rich *logical* ambiguity of that last line (centring upon the elliptical 'therefore' and 'because') points to another of the methods by which authenticity of utterance is won – and here we approach the elements of transfigured 'peculiarity' in Donne's 'normative' poetry, the particular, inherited, perceptual bias which made him himself and no one else. In all the lines quoted so far, the animating vigour has been very much bound up with the following out of an argument, with acts of definition, analogies, syllogisms. 'Their attempts were always analytick', as Johnson observed of the metaphysical poets: it is a truth at once obvious and difficult to interpret.

The analytic method, for Donne, is not one poetic tactic amongst many, but the necessary form for a mental operation which is one of *hammering out* a meaning ('Wit's forge and fire-blast', as Coleridge puts it). The poetry demands that we shall be aware of logical structure. But not as enforcing conclusions. The logical rigour both implements, and expresses, a rigour more comprehensive than the logical – a rigour which is determined to lay hold intellectually upon its experience. You could almost say that logic, in Donne, is a sustained metaphor for intellectual perseverance, which it subserves. So that the force of the word 'therefore' in the last line of 'Twicknam Garden' lies, not in its winding up of the syllogism – there is in fact *no* syllogism – but in its anguished rendering of a state of feeling so contradictory as to defy all logic (the defiance making up much of the anguish, and the persevering logical effort figuring the refusal to give in to the anguish). And in a similar way, analogical structure in the argument of 'A Lecture upon the Shadow' (Love, like the sun, is either growing or constant) serves mainly as a prelude to the breakdown of the analogy (but, unlike the sun, it has no gradual decline: after noon, comes immediate, total, and devastating eclipse). The breakdown dramatises the frightening discontinuity between natural expectation and the real conditions of love, and the persisting will-to-analogy reveals Donne's determination to keep cool in the crisis.

Occasionally the logic meets no checks from an incoercible reality; and then the sense of accumulating power in the relentless self-contemplation is astonishing. In the following lines from 'A Nocturnall upon S. Lucies Day', Donne is steadily closing, and locking, every door that might conceivably lead out of his imprisoning nihilistic despair; but the logical progression, while overtly 'proving' his nothingness, is actually objectifying and dramatising his fierce refusal of false comfort in a situation which holds no comfort. The grip Donne is maintaining upon his despair gives rise to an unbroken chain of syllogisms, all leading to the conclusion – delayed till the last moment – that 'I am None':

> Were I a man, that I were one,
> I needs must know; I should preferre,
>   If I were any beast,
> Some ends, some means; Yea plants, yea stones detest,
> And love; All, all some properties invest;
> If I an ordinary nothing were,
> As shadow, a light, and body must be here.
>
> *But I am None*; nor will my Sunne renew.

There's no gainsaying the clangour and authenticity of disgust and despair in that climatic cry – except perhaps by pointing out that the vigour of mind which drives the logic to its terrible conclusion, and the resilience of wit which can find, even there, something sourly amusing about its own subhuman torpor, are signs that the nullity, the nightmare insubstantiality which has gripped him, is beginning to dissolve in the very act of apprehending it. That is the poem's triumph over the unmeaning it deals in.

In what sense, though, is this a matter of 'life' – for that is the account I'm proposing of the authority this voice carries within itself? Just as there is a certain thinness of tone which comes from holding forth in areas too remote from one's own living concerns, so there is a fullness and richness of tone which is available only to the man who speaks out of the heart of his experience. As a species we are much given to lying, to the erection of false fronts around our private and emotional lives, to the invention of social tones which will pass conventionally for candour, but which actually spell the death of all candour. Donne's distinction is that, lacking what one might call the Wordsworthian resource – that great spring of unexhausted naturalness which could well up and inundate mere mental consciousness – he nevertheless invented ways, conscious ways, of creating his candour. It is a 'technique for sincerity',[1] a discipline for the possessing of experience.

It is as a part of that discipline that the acts of intellectual appropriation so characteristic of the poetry are to be understood. That is why, as Donne's mind moves in to take possession, the authoritativeness grows. We are given states, apparently of total prostration, like the 'Nocturnall', and yet the effect is not one of disintegration, but of concentration. Even when, in 'A Hymne to God the Father', Donne articulates his most unmanning fears, and submits to a God who is clearly one of them, one can still hear that strong, fearless, composed voice ringing out:

> I have a sinn of feare that when I have spunn
> My last thred, I shall perish on the shore;
> Sweare by thy self that at my Death, thy Sunn
> Shall shine as it shines now, and heretofore;
> And having done that, thou hast done,
> I have noe more.

That, I suggest, is the same voice we heard in 'The Sunne Rising': the exultancy and the fear have something very deep in common. One hears, in both, the voice of a man who will not be shaken loose from his standing, will not be betrayed into the frivolous or the defensive or the pompous, the peripherally witty or the centrally soggy emotion no matter what threats to his composure – ecstatic, grievous or despairing – may present themselves.

It would be doing nobody a service, least of all Donne, to push this analysis any further in the direction of formula. These poems, even the dismembered fragments of them I've been able to discuss in a short space, offer us new realities 'for the honour of human nature', new embodied meanings, in the great common contexts, for human dignity. It is enough to go on with.

I have been speaking of this major quality in Donne as if it were something that was likely to strike the reader on a first acquaintance. But of course the critical problem we began by confronting only arises be-

[1] Dr Leavis uses the phrase of Eliot's poetic development (*Lectures in America* (1969), p. 40). The comparison with Donne is a very pertinent one.

cause it may not. It depends where he happens to open his volume. Statistically speaking, he is equally likely to be struck at first by a callous pertness:

> Chang'd loves are but chang'd sorts of meat,
> And when hee hath the kernell eate,
> Who doth not fling away the shell?
> ('Communitie')

Or by something that used, in more discreet ages, to be called grossness, and which even in our own looks like a parade of cheap emancipation:

> Rich Nature hath in women wisely made
> Two purses, and their mouths aversely laid:
> They then, which to the lower tribute owe,
> That way which that Exchequer looks, must go.
> ('Elegie 18: Loves Progress')

By laborious pedantry offering itself as perception:

> You that are she and you, that's double shee,
> In her dead face, halfe of your selfe shall see;
> Shee was the other part, for so they doe
> Which build them friendships, become one of two;
> So two, that but themselves no third can fit,
> Which were to be so, when they were not yet...
> ('Verse Letter: To the Lady Bedford')

or as piety:

> Loe, where condemned hee
> Beares his owne crosse, with paine, yet by and by
> When it beares him, he must beare more and die.
> ('La Corona, 5')

Such manifestations would seem to be quite adequately covered by Dr Johnson's dismissive phrase – 'perverseness of industry'; unless 'perversion' is the word – perversion of those qualities of daring, fearlessness, acuity, and perseverance that one applauds elsewhere in Donne. However uncomfortably we may grant it, the characteristic impress of this very individual mind is as visible here as in the more respectable poems. Perhaps more visible, because the idiosyncratic is not sustained by any real originality and the cleverness has very little of intelligence about it. It is pure Clevelandism.

The time has now come to lay the formal charges – or rather, to let Johnson do it for us. I give the central passage from the *Life of Cowley* in full, not only because it is a classic of critical clarity and acumen, but also because the prose grounds its vigour upon the infinitely resourceful pursuit of an argumentative *sequence*. To grasp that sequence is to recognise how much more than a poetic manner, more even than an intellectual habit, Johnson is deploring. The aberrations he castigates – which are those we have been noting – imply a total attitude to the common body of human experience, and it is that attitude he brands as 'improper and vicious'.

If wit be well described by Pope, as being 'that which has been often thought, but was never before so well expressed', they certainly never attained, nor ever sought it; for they endeavoured to be singular in their thoughts, and were careless of their diction. But Pope's account of wit is undoubtedly erroneous: he depresses it below its natural dignity, and reduces it from strength of thought to happiness of language.

If by a more noble and more adequate conception that be considered as wit which is at once natural and new, that which, though not obvious, is, upon its first production, acknowledged to be just; if it be that which he that never found it wonders how he missed; to wit of this kind the metaphysical poets have seldom risen. Their thoughts are often new, but seldom natural; they are not obvious, but neither are they just; and the reader, far from wondering that he missed them, wonders more frequently by what perverseness of industry they were ever found.

But wit, abstracted from its effects upon the hearer, may be more rigorously and philosophically considered as a kind of *discordia concors*; a combination of dissimilar images, or discovery of occult resemblances in things apparently unlike. Of wit, thus defined, they have more than enough. The most heterogeneous ideas are yoked by violence together; nature and art are ransacked for illustrations, comparisons, and allusions; their learning instructs, and their subtlety surprises; but the reader commonly thinks his improvement dearly bought, and, though he sometimes admires, is seldom pleased.

From this account of their compositions it will be readily inferred, that they were not successful in representing or moving the affections. As they were wholly employed on something unexpected and surprising, they had no regard to that uniformity of sentiment which enables us to conceive and to excite the pains and the pleasure of other minds: they never inquired what, on any occasion, they should have said or done; but wrote rather as beholders than partakers of human nature; as beings looking upon good and evil, impassive and at leisure: as Epicurean deities, making remarks on the actions of men, and the vicissitudes of life, without interest and without emotion. Their courtship was void of fondness, and their lamentation of sorrow. Their wish was only to say what they hoped had never been said before.

Nor was the sublime more within their reach than the pathetick; for they never attempted that comprehension and expanse of thought which at once fills the whole mind, and of which the first effect is sudden astonishment, and the second rational admiration. Sublimity is produced by aggregation, and littleness by dispersion. Great thoughts are always general, and consist in positions not limited by exceptions, and in descriptions not descending to minuteness. It is with great propriety that subtlety, which in its original import means exility of particles, is taken in its metaphorical meaning for nicety of distinction. Those writers who lay on the watch for novelty could have little hope of greatness; for great things cannot have escaped former observation. Their attempts were always analytick; they broke every image into fragments; and could no more represent, by their slender conceits and laboured particularities, the prospects of nature, or the scenes of life, than he who dissects a sun-beam with a prism can exhibit the wide effulgence of a summer noon.

What they wanted however of the sublime, they endeavoured to supply by hyperbole; their amplification had no limits; they left not only reason but fancy behind them; and produced combinations of confused magnificence, that not only could not be credited, but could not be imagined.

The diagnosis is of a persistent indifference to, or contempt for, 'the hearer', a neglect of 'the pains and pleasure of other minds', and an affected 'beholding' of that 'human nature' in which one can only be a 'partaker'. That is the human significance of what Coleridge called 'intenseness and peculiarity of thought'. Johnson wants it called 'perverseness'.

'Critical Remarks are not easily understood without examples', and the examples Johnson draws from Donne do a good deal to illuminate the general case. For two-thirds of his examples of the 'improper and vicious' he goes to the *Verse Letters*, the *Epicedes and Obsequies*, the *Epithalamions* – in short, to the territories of moral discourse most neglected by modern readers. This may appear to let us off the hook: Johnson, poor chap, read the wrong poems. But apart from his fastening, often, upon the more interesting moments in those poems, he also selects for reprehension passages from three of the most admired *Songs and Sonets*. And when one asks oneself why he is unable to see the merit of the poetry that lies under his pen, the answer seems to be less that

he was a purblind denizen of the Age of Reason, than that he is read-
ing them as if they were written by the same poet who devised the
ingenious absurdities he derides in the *Epithalamions, Verse Letters,
Elegies* and so on. We, on the other hand, tend to read the *Songs and
Sonets* as if they were written by some different and quite unconnected
poet, assuming, in effect, some essential discontinuity in the *oeuvre*.
But is that quite faithful to the experience of reading Donne?

Not if Coleridge's wryly-noted misgivings are at all representative:

> With Donne, whose muse on dromedary trots,
> Wreathe iron pokers into true-love knots;
> Rhyme's sturdy cripple, fancy's maze and clue;
> Wit's forge and fire-blast, meaning's press and screw.[1]

The blend of exasperation and admiration – exasperation reluctantly
yielding to admiration – which is so excellently caught here, if it is at
all an accurate register of the poetry, forbids us to bifurcate the wit of
Donne into 'ingenious absurdity' on the one hand, and 'intenseness
and peculiarity of thought' on the other. The means express the end.
The strength and skill required to convert pokers into love-knots is
exerted because love-knots are conceived to be not altogether unlike
pokers. If Donne is a cripple of rhyme, he is a distinctly 'sturdy' one,
and in need of no assistance from the Guardians of the poetic Poor.
And when Coleridge chooses a metaphor from the smith's art, he
shows himself thoroughly in sympathy with Donne's mind – a mind
for which nothing less than forge and fire-blast can be relied upon to
elicit meaning. The manner, in other words, is not for Coleridge, any
more than it was for Johnson, a detachable personal quirk: it reflects a
total view of the nature of meaning, its location, and the method of
extracting it ('press and screw'). The bewilderingly labyrinthine in
the poetic strategy is not just 'fancy's maze': it also contains fancy's
'clue'; and the clue is to be found only in the maze. The idiosyncrasy
is a condition of the greatness. Upon the idiosyncrasy, therefore, we
begin.

It's not surprising, given the view of Donne sketched in his verse-
impromptu, that 'The Canonization' was, for Coleridge, 'one of my
favourite poems'. Certainly it is a piece which gives ample substance

[1] R. F. Brinkley (ed.), *Coleridge on the Seventeeth Century* (1955), p. 526.

to the metaphor of a maze, and one which holds out to its reader continuous tantalising suggestions that there lies, somewhere within it, the clue. It constitutes a useful reminder, too, that if we are to locate the 'natural' and the 'just', what one might call the organising centres of the poetry's seriousness, it will not be done by setting up seriousness as the antithesis of wit. For 'The Canonization' combines an extreme earnestness of overt content with a disconcerting frivolity of manner, and what we need to discover, in order to read it at all, is some way round the crude dichotomy between the serious and the flippant.

But what, with the best will in the world, is one to make of the tone of this stanza (the question moved is the status of the two lovers)?

> Call us what you will, wee are made such by love;
> Call her one, mee another flye,
> We'are Tapers too, and at our own cost die,
> And wee in us finde the'Eagle and the Dove.
> The Phoenix ridle hath more wit
> By us, we two being one, are it.
> So to one neutrall thing both sexes fit,
> Wee dye and rise the same, and prove
> Mysterious by this love.

The first oddity that strikes the ear is that curious, mincing dryness of tone ('we two being one, are it') which, beside the straightforward masculine vigour of the opening ('For Godsake hold your tongue, and let me love...'), has a tantalising air of prim self-parody (or was it the 'straightforward masculine vigour' that was being parodied? – it is very much the kind of poem to provoke such puzzled queries). We are of course amused, but the amusement proves not to be of the kind that we can comfortably rest in.

We are first tempted to take 'straight' the resentful shrugging off of unsought meddling ('and at our *owne* cost die'), though the faintly sulky note ('I can't see what concern of *yours* it is') is disquieting; and then this is offset by the sanctimonious complacency of 'And wee in us finde the'Eagle and the Dove', which is surely self-deflating – the close proximity of the two pronouns ('wee in us') seems bent on drawing attention to the acute isolation of the loving pair and questioning very much, as a consequence, any valuation made from within the tight circle of that first person plural. The upshot, by the time we get to 'prove/Mysterious by this love', is that 'Mysterious' has come to sound bottomlessly equivocal: the momentous line-end pause on 'prove' imparts an unctuous parsonical tremolo to the word so that we can't be sure in what spirit it is offered. A spirit of mystification perhaps? The basic poetic strategy, at all events, seems to be to defy all attempts to ascertain the seriousness of the claims to sanctity.

That goes not only for the exorbitant substance of the claims, nor for the equivocal manner merely, but also for the grounds alleged – because Donne appears to argue the quasi-divine status of the lovers on the preposterous grounds that they re-enact the resurrection of Christ ('Wee dye and rise the same'). And that proposition, of course, rests on a pun – no less excruciating for its shop-soiled condition – on the secondary meaning of 'dye' (to pass away in sexual ecstasy). He is thus impertinently confounding mere carnality with a prime mystery of religion. Nor does the poem as a whole provide much guidance to the interpretation of this blasphemous witticism, for it ends on the same uninterpretable note of rhapsodic unction as this stanza:

> Beg from above
> A patterne of your love!

It's perfectly obvious that this is a highly 'serious' poem – at least in what it undertakes. But it's equally obvious that the seriousness is to be located in no single tone, or formulation, or image. Those lightning shifts of tone, from the bland to the sombre ('Call us what you will, wee are made such by love'), or from the pert to the profound ('Wee dye and rise the same, and prove/Mysterious...'), pull the carpet from under our feet. And the verse movement, which is at once flightily restive *and* crisp and flat, suggests a mind which extraordinarily combines agile hyperactivity with a drily ironic self-awareness. 'Seriousness' in short – the quality we set out in search of – is so consistently deflected by a restive self-consciousness, that we are forced to put the word in inverted commas and follow it with a question mark.

It is the very possibility of seriousness that the poem is questioning. The title ('The Canonization') implies straight away a disposition to push the 'religion of love' over the brink into the exaggeration and absurdity it always borders upon: it takes with mock literal-mindedness what has, by constant iteration, ceased to be an active metaphor, and so queries its fitness – just what is the status of these saints in the Church of Venus? how holy are love's 'mysteries'? is the amorous solipsism of the mutually absorbed lovers a religious retreat into the 'peace' of love by which they are 'Made one anothers hermitage? or is it an act of withdrawal so complete as to constitute a withdrawal from life ('Wee can dye by it, if not *live* by love')? The disconcerting play of tones – magnanimous then wry, scoffing and then mock-pompous – in short, the *wit* which takes into consideration so many possible attitudes to the same phenomenon, is Donne's way of exploring his own seriousness. And if the seriousness is to be located anywhere, it will be in the wit.

Well and good. But the mental operations in 'The Canonization' that are most obviously witty, seem the operations of a very uneasy mind. I'll be noting more than once how fond Donne is of inviting the reader's complicity in the activities of chronic self-consciousness, and how frequently he has to have recourse to the hypothetical votary or voyeur, the watching eye of the external world, before he can give any substance to his love. His wit is very often an extension of that self-conscious unease – the secret, zigzagging flight of a mind determined to throw all pursuers off the scent. To be perpetually uncertain whether you mean what you say or not, perpetually trying on new roles and discarding them; to be always using your hearer as a sounding-board to test your seriousness, to be finally incapable of direct, unironic statement, is to be the victim of a psychic disorder which may claim pity but hardly deserves veneration. It is just a sad kind of intellectual hypochondria, a state of self-absorption so acute that the sufferer can enter into relation with nothing external to himself.

The usual critical resource, at this point, is to invoke, somewhat anachronistically, the ubiquitous and ever-ready *persona*. This is not, we are informed with mild scorn, Donne speaking here, but his persona; and the pursuit of the poem's real voice, its centre of consciousness, is therefore the pursuit of a phantom. One might make several retorts to this elucidation of the problem: one is that the sense of being induced to pursue a phantom is precisely what makes this verse disquieting, and giving a literary name to the sport doesn't make it any more enjoyable. Another is that self-exploratory role-playing of one kind or another is a constant feature of Donne's poetry, and it doesn't always assume this elusive character. One might also add parenthetically that the word 'persona' implies a relationship between the self that creates the poem, and the self that is created in the poem, which comes perilously close to being an imaginative dislocation – a collapse of psychic integrity. But the crucial matter, when it is Donne we are considering, is that the use of a persona for such purposes would constitute a betrayal of that speech from the heart of experience, that achieved candour, for which he is so remarkable. Instead of the utterance of 'a naked thinking heart' – this is the charge – we are getting the prepared speeches of a fully-clothed, plotting persona, speeches it is impossible to read quite 'as one reads the living' because there is an equivocation as to whether the speaker is really there at all. The persona, in short, is a concept only required when one detects some disjunction between the creating intelligence and the intelligence created, and one finds oneself, as reader, consequently, held at arm's length by the poetry. That is the poetic quality in (and, one suspects, the personal predicament behind) Marvell's 'Definition of Love'. It is not the quality of the greatest Donne.

'The Canonization' is not exactly a Marvell poem inadvertently composed by Donne: the wit is too spirited for that, the possible good humour too probable (though you can never actually lay your hand on it). But something of the suspicion does attach to the poem. One is very conscious of the deployment of wit, but never sure what it is being deployed upon – or at whose expense. The 'subject' recedes as one approaches and vanishes when one tries to grasp it – unless of course the subject is 'wit' and the enlarged cheek has been designed expressly for Donne to put his tongue in it. But to call this total activity Wit (returning again to that mine of wisdom, the *Life of Cowley*) 'depresses it below its natural dignity, and reduces it from strength of thought to happiness of language'. That indeed is the trouble with a great deal of the talk one hears about 'the wit of Donne': it implies an acute lack of material patched over and eked out with displays of verbal sophistication.

The tinkling of urbane cymbals is irritating enough in life, and there is no reason why we should tolerate it any more in poetry. Without an informing 'strength of thought', wit becomes a matter of pretty marginal interest. But

if, by a more noble and more adequate conception that be considered as wit which is at once natural and new, that which, though not obvious, is, upon its first production, acknowledged to be just; if it be that which he that never found it wonders how he missed; to wit of this kind

(Johnson can only be encountered on his own ground), to wit of this kind Donne has, at times, magnificently risen. But we shall not grasp the importance of those occasions until we have attended carefully to the strictures of Johnson, and of all the subsequent detractors who have paraphrased him. They refuse, quite rightly, to concern themselves with 'the wit of Donne' as a quality peculiar to that poet. That it *is* peculiar to him is precisely what they complain of. What they are interested in, is the way that wit bears upon the human world they share with Donne – where it is 'natural' and where 'just', how it displays 'strength of thought' and no mere 'happiness of language'. The questions have obvious force and deserve a cogent answer.

My first response would be to direct attention away from problematical pieces like 'The Canonization', to other of the *Songs and Sonets* – say, 'The Anniversiare' or 'A Valediction: forbidding Mourning' – poems that so wholly seize the imagination one stops thinking in terms of problems and solutions. And with these poems, significantly, the question of there being a persona never even arises, and one is fairly soon casting about for a word with a larger human content, a greater implicit range of felt experience, than 'wit'. The wit remains a part of the poetic experience, but one is prompted to talk more about the quality of the love celebrated than about the condition of the celebrating mind.

But there is, as well, a whole range of Donne's poetry, an important colour-range on his spectrum, where one needs the term 'wit'. And some of this is not to be accounted for as an imperfect approximation to the larger humanity of the greater poetry. It is, very enjoyably, something different. The wit may not manifest exactly 'strength of thought', but it does have remarkable vivacity of thought, and it can be cleared of the charge of being self-enclosed, narcissistic, sealed up in its own self-consciousness.

I'm thinking here of the early Donne – the best of the *Satyres,* a few *Elegies,* and the prose *Paradoxes* – products of an obviously young, resilient, and vivacious mind. They are none of them pieces one is likely to revisit over the years with a deep and growing admiration, but they are an engaging reminder that wit, besides being all the eminent things Johnson says it is, can also be extremely funny. One would never call 'The Canonization' 'funny': wit there has become itself something of a problem. But in Donne's early writings the witty high spirits are unconstrained. They may seem at first, indeed, a little showy, indulged too much for their own sake. So they are. Donne is at that rapturous stage of development when the discharge of native energy is its own complete justification. He has that deliberate, yet oddly selfless egocentricity of a young man utterly confident of his powers and profoundly indifferent to his future. So that one comes to sense, in the very irresponsibility of the wit, an indispensable responsive vitality: he is revelling in the joys of a robust, unintimidated ego.

Interestingly enough, the early work includes, scattered among the *Paradoxes*, something that looks rather like an *ad hoc* philosophy of wit, a theoretical trellis knocked together for the luxuriance of wit to climb upon. It provides a good frame, too, for our consideration of the *Satyres* and *Elegies*, and a useful beginning for another chapter.

2

'Heterogeneous ideas' and 'unexpected truth' –
Paradoxes and Problemes, Satyres, Elegies

Wit, in Donne's early writing, is very much a laughing matter. If we were so unguardedly pompous as to demand a justification for all the immoderate mirth, Donne's answer would probably be some impenitent epigram like 'Paradox 10' – 'That a Wise Man is knowne by much laughing'. It's vain, of course, to ask the propounder of such paradoxes if he 'really means it': he will only laugh, and try to get you to do the same, thus proving himself entirely in earnest about the importance of laughter. And yet there's no doubt that the perceptions activated to produce our laughter involve quite delicate operations of intelligence. Indeed it's as an *expression* of intelligence that Donne is interested in laughter.

If thou beest *wise, laugh*: for since the *powers* of *discourse, reason,* and *laughter,* bee equally *proper* unto Man onely, why shall not hee be onely most *wise,* which hath most use of *laughing,* as well as he which hath most of *reasoning* and *discoursing*? I alwaies did, and shall understand that *Adage*...That by much *laughing* thou maist know there is a *foole,* not, that the *laughers* are *fooles,* but that among them there is some *foole,* at whome *wisemen* laugh.

And at the same time as he anatomises the act of laughter, Donne is inviting our collaboration in it, as an activity properly shared by 'wisemen'. Fools can't be expected to join in, for they're not only 'the most laughed at', they also 'laugh the least themselves of any'. Laughter, then, is a sign of wisdom, and not least because it avoids the excesses of over-reaction that folly tends to provoke – reactions like envy, pity, anger – offering instead an intelligent sublimation of our emotions and resentments:

A *foole* if he come into a *Princes Court*, and see a *gay* man leaning at the wall, so *glistering*, and so *painted* in many *colours* that he is hardly discerned from one of the *pictures* in the *Arras* hanging, his *body* like an *Iron-bound-chest*, girt in and thicke ribb'd with *broad gold laces*, may (and commonly doth) envy him. But alas! shall a *wiseman*, which may not onely not *envy*, but not *pitty* this *monster*, do nothing? Yes, let him *laugh*. And if one of these *hot cholerike firebrands*, which nourish themselves by *quarrelling*, and kindling others, spit upon a *foole* one *spark* of *disgrace*, he, like a *thatcht house* quickly burning, may bee *angry*; but the *wiseman*, as *cold* as the *Salamander*, may not onely not be *angry* with him, but not be *sorry* for him; therefore let him *laugh*: so he shall be knowne a Man, because he can *laugh*, a *wise Man* that hee knowes at *what* to laugh, and a *valiant Man*, that he *dares* laugh...

The position is as serious as a philosophy of laughter can reasonably be, though Donne is quick to warn us that we recognise its truth only by laughing at it:

and to shew themselves in *promptnesse* of *laughing* is so great in *wisemen*, that I thinke all *wisemen*, if any *wiseman* do reade this *Paradox*, will *laugh* both at it and me.

That final, limber twist of dialectic is pure Donne – the activities of wit themselves occasion further witty activity; and what might have been a dismal example of the egocentric spiral of constricting self-consciousness (the self observing the self observing the self, in a wilderness of mirrors none of which contains the true image of the self) broadens out into a shared amusement at the absurdities inherent in self-consciousness. He so positively enjoys his own mental agility, finds such a fund of inexhaustible energy there, that self-consciousness itself can be taken up into the continually renewing processes of wit. And the wit is collaborative not exclusive.

There is a further advantage in approaching Donne the satirist by way of the *Paradoxes*: we can see how far his wit is from being a mere freak of temperament, something peculiar to himself – or, if it was that, how thoroughly it has been built into the foundations of a coherent (paradoxically coherent, anyway) view of life. When Donne looks at Nature he sees something rather like Wordsworth's version of Bartholomew Fair – 'a parliament of monsters'. But the use of this extraordinary phenomenon is immediately obvious to him, as it wasn't to Wordsworth:

Nature saw this *faculty* [of laughing] to bee so necessary in man, that shee hath beene content that by *more causes* we should be importuned to *laugh*, than to the *exercise* of any other power...   ('Paradox 10')

Now, the point of invoking 'Nature' in this way, is that Donne sees his own satirical activity not so much as an accusation against Nature, as a participation in it. For, in the words of 'Paradox 3', 'by Discord things increase' – the implication of which declaration for a writer of paradoxes, does not escape him either:

...I assevere this the more boldly, because while I maintain it, and feele the *Contrary repugnancies* and *adverse fightings* of the *Elements* in my body, my Body increaseth; and whilst I differ from common opinions by this *Discord*, the number of my *Paradoxes* increaseth.

And indeed, if we were to ask what kind of general philosophical position would accommodate and nourish the energetically robust vision of life that we get in Donne's early verse and prose, it would clearly have to be something of this kind: a vitality exulting in the 'Contrary repugnancies and adverse fightings of the Elements' and, even when they take place in one's own body, feeling them to be a natural and enjoyable part of the body's 'increase'. It is a vitality for which Concord must necessarily seem flat, tame and unprofitable:

Discord is never so barren that it affords no fruit; for the *fall* of one *estate* is at the worst the *increaser* of another, because it is as impossible to finde a *discommodity* without *advantage*, as to finde *Corruption* without *Generation*: But it is the *Nature* and *Office* of *Concord* to *preserve* onely...

A philosophy, in short, for which the natural strife of things, 'the *Discord* of *Extreames*' which 'begets all vertues', is preferable to any kind of harmony that can be imagined superimposed upon it. And the man of intelligence is to be found, in the midst of all the rude anarchic discharge of energy, living, not by his wits, but by his Wit – that most miraculous organ which transmutes the chaos of nature into food and sustenance. Wit is both a product and a continuation of the great creative strife.

I need hardly point out how strikingly at odds this is with the vision of Nature as Order, which all self-respecting Elizabethans are supposed to have taken for granted. That it *is* at odds with received opinion is, of course, partly Donne's reason for espousing it so enthusiastically. Yet the critique, in its own modestly flippant way,

goes deeper than a shallow rebelliousness. It is pragmatic at precisely
the point where the philosophies of Order are not. Reality – Donne is
quite clear about this – is not to be located in some invisible, spiritual
world, but in the visible physical one. And the contention of 'Paradox
11' is 'That the gifts of the body are better than those of the mind'.
One of his chief arguments in defence of this monstrous doctrine is
that the realm of invisible essences, qualities and virtues is subject to
the most drastic misconstructions; whereas appearances are always
what they seem, and therefore to be trusted: Platonism stood on its
head. Anyway, he goes on, 'the *soule* it seemes is enabled by our *body,*
not this by it'. The virtues themselves have their cause in the body
rather than the mind (those who doubt it are referred to 'Physitians'
for corroboration). It is a 'Paradox' of course, but one which is much
more than a calculated outrage on received ideas: it's a spirited at-
tempt to meet the formlessness of the phenomenal world without
transcendental evasion, and at the same time to give the inevitable
laughter of the wise man some solid standing upon the nature of
reality.

The most obvious application of this energetic pragmatism comes
in the matter of love, where poor human beings have been much
tormented by spiritualising humbugs hawking ideals incapable of
realisation. The solution, plainly, as Donne explains in the first and
best of the *Paradoxes,* is to embrace with joyous cynicism the real
woman. The pursuit of an imaginary ideal harmony merely makes the
pursuer deaf to the delectable discord of the reality:

This name of *Inconstancy,* which hath so much beene poysoned with slaunders,
ought to bee changed into *variety,* for the which the world is so delightful, *and
a Woman for that the most delightfull thing in this world.*

It is perverse to do anything but exult in this peculiarly female
quality:

Are not your wits pleased with those jests, which coozen your expectation?
You can call it Pleasure to be beguil'd in troubles, and in the most excellent
toy in the world, you call it Treachery: I would you had your *Mistresses* so
constant, that they would never change, no not so much as their *smocks,* then
should you see what sluttish vertue, *Constancy* were. *Inconstancy* is a most com-
mendable and cleanly quality, and Women in this quality are farre more
absolute than the Heavens, than the Starres, Moone, or any thing beneath it;
for long observation hath pickt certainety out of their mutability....

The only men who are so besotted with constancy as to libel Woman for her inconstancy are the fusty old didacts, incapable of any zestful participation in life, whom it is the distinction of Woman to take down a peg or two.

Every Woman is a *Science*; for hee that plods upon a Woman all his life long, shall at length find himselfe short of the knowledge of her: they are borne to take downe the pride of wit, and ambition of wisedome, making *fooles* wise in the advertising to winne them, *wisemen* fooles in conceit of losing their labours; witty men starke mad, being confounded with their uncertaineties. *Philosophers* write against them for spite, not desert, that having attained to some knowledge in all other things, in them onely they know nothing, but are meerely ignorant: *Active* and *Experienced* men raile against them, because they love in their livelesse and decrepit age, when all goodnesse leaves them. These envious *Libellers* ballad against them, because having nothing in themselves able to deserve their love, they maliciously discommend all they cannot obtaine, thinking to make men beleeve they know much, because they are able to dispraise much, and rage against *Inconstancy*, when they were never admitted into so much favour as to be forsaken. In mine Opinion such men are happy that Women are *Inconstant*, for so may they chance to bee beloved of some excellent Women (when it comes to their turne) out of their *Inconstancy* and mutability, though not out of their owne desert.

This is a secular hymn in praise of the actual. The actual, you might object, rather shallowly conceived; which is true. But it's not so much the philosophical postures struck here (and elsewhere in the *Paradoxes*) that concern me – and let it be granted they *are* 'struck' – as the bent of mind they render more intelligible. There is a characteristic movement in Donne's poetry which starts off wryly contemplating the realm of ideal beauties and ideal joys ('This, no to morrow hath, nor yesterday...'), yet comes to rest with a full and foreseen satisfaction upon a much more limited yet richer actuality ('this is the second of our raigne'). A simple example is the anti-climatic opening of 'Elegie 11: The Bracelet':

> Not that in colour it was like thy haire,
> For Armelets of that thou maist let me weare:
> Nor that thy hand it oft embrac'd and kist,
> For so it had that good, which oft I mist:
> Nor for that silly old moralitie,
> That as those linkes were knit, our love should bee:

> Mourne I that I thy seavenfold chaine have lost;
> Nor for the luck sake; but the bitter cost.

That is not – what it might appear – realism of the shallow kind that pounces gleefully upon the disreputable motivation in order to wreak misanthropic vengeance on an all-too-vulnerable world of sentiment. No bony finger of accusation is pointed. The laugh it elicits from us is one of self-recognition and genial acceptance, as remote as may be from cynicism and misanthropy: 'Ah, poor mortals! we would be loftier if we might, but alas!...the bitter cost!' The mind comes to rest, with an unmistakable humorous ease, upon the simple, the base feeling. So that the feeling ceases to be base. The lost chain, in the rest of the 'Elegie', becomes the representative of all those petty frustrations which threaten our good sense and good humour, tempting us into melodrama, and about which the wise man must find ways of laughing. The meanly actual is only mean while we are trying to wish it away; accepted, it takes on a kind of genial reality.

It is a small example of something that goes a long way toward making Donne a more than 'witty' poet – a good-humoured acceptance of human limitation, mellowing at times into the ripe awareness that it is much better that things should be so. At its most mature it gives us lines as fine as those richly anti-climactic ones which open 'Loves Growth':

> I scarce beleeve my love to be so pure
>   As I had thought it was,
>   Because it doth endure
> Vicissitude, and season, as the grasse;
> Me thinkes I lyed all winter, when I swore,
> My love was infinite, if spring make' it more.

The living, growing reality is so much more satisfying than the static perfections of infinity which a barren love-idealism could propose. 'All flesh is grass,' intones the ascetic, directing the novice to the higher love. 'Yes,' replies Donne, 'and have you ever noticed how beautiful grass is!' The acceptance of the actual is founded upon a faith in the endlessness of the natural – a faith in love's *growth*.

But that is leaping a long way ahead. At present we are trying to find a way into the *Satyres* and *Elegies*, poems which seem to find the natural and the actual to consist mainly of the preposterous.

Laughter for Donne, as we have seen, is an act of participation, not of withdrawal. There can be about his satire none of that censorious complacency, making invidious exception for himself, which often makes the satirist ridiculous in ways he clearly hasn't envisaged. To exercise one's wit is to plunge right into the midst of the 'Contrary repugnancies and adverse fightings of the Elements'; and no artificial immunity can be claimed there. But the effect of thus plunging in is to invite a particular kind of collaboration from the audience – and I'm thinking now especially of the *Satyres*. The nearest anaolgy for the implicit social 'tone' would be the party wit who has collected a group of listeners, but has not yet lapsed into showing off for their benefit. He has just as warm an appreciation of the intelligence and alertness of his audience, as the audience has of his wit; and the wit therefore contains a tacit understanding that anybody present might be making the jokes, though *he* happens just now to be the agreed spokesman for the corporate high spirits. It is, in terms of a useful distinction of Johnson's, not 'gaiety', but 'good-humour':

Gaiety is to good-humour as animal perfumes to vegetable fragrance; the one overpowers weak spirits, and the other recreates and revives them. Gaiety seldom fails to give some pain; the hearers either strain their faculties to accompany its towerings, or are left behind in envy and despair. Good-humour boasts no faculties which every one does not believe in his own power...[1]

It is, however, a danger game for which everything is in question, nothing is sacred, and the only obligation is the obligation not to be dull. The voice – in turn that of improviser, mimic, censor or buffoon – is given us in all its twists and turns as it wheedles, regales, shocks, and then tickles its audience. It is inescapably a performance; and that is the explanation of the rhythmical peculiarities that most readers are struck by, and many of them obstructed by, in the *Satyres* – the 'rough' metre, the muse on dromedary trotting.

Of course it isn't merely rough: this is not a case of a poet of fallible ear imperfectly foreseeing the way he wants his lines to be spoken. The *Satyres* are meticulously scored for the speaking voice and there is usually only one way of saying the lines. The difficulty is to find that one way. As Coleridge has it,

To read Dryden, Pope, &c., you need only count syllables; but to read Donne you must measure *Time*, and discover the *Time* of each word by the sense of

[1] *Rambler* No. 72.

Passion. I would ask no surer test of a Scotchman's *substratum* (for the turf-cover of pretension they all have) than to make him read Donne's satires aloud. If he made manly metre of them and yet strict metre, then, – why, then he wasn't a Scotchman, or his soul was geographically slandered by his body's first appearing there.[1]

Metrically the verse may seem a very unstable compound: with a sovereign indifference to prosodic decorum Donne has crammed the most slipshod of colloquial rhythms – cadences heavily slurred and elided, with anything up to four syllables in a single foot – into a pedantically finger-ticking five-beat line. But the packed and chaotic quality that results is a working quality: it lends itself splendidly to an excitable, super-stimulated rhetoric, exceedingly emphatic stresses, and a very broad range of expressive inflexion – everything from an exasperated shriek to a lugubrious growl. The crowding of syllables suggests an impetuous improviser, and the imposition (by a whisker) of last-minute metrical order shows the improviser's mastery pitting itself successfully against the necessary formal impediment which gives zest to the performance. The rhythmic mode is excellently fitted, too, to the vocal mimicry with which the *Satyres* abound. The 'fondling motley humorist', Donne's street companion in 'Satyre 1', makes a leg to a passing dandy, and Donne bursts out,

> But Oh, God strengthen thee, why stoop'st thou so?
> Why? he hath travayld; Long? No; but to me
> (Which understand none,) he doth seeme to be
> Perfect French, and Italian; I replyed,
> So is the Poxe.

The mimicry is not directed merely at the satiric butts, but also at the satirist whose fat, phlegmatic complacency is elegantly caught in that last 'knock-down' retort. The raconteur is unconsciously drama-tising himself – as in the earlier spluttering tirade against the incon-stancy of the 'humorist'. Donne has already warned him that he does not intend to be left stranded in the middle street – 'For better or worse *take* me, or *leave mee*:/To take *and* leave mee is a*dul*tery' (and notice how the thundering stresses are giving us the staring exaspera-tion of the speaker) – and he has extorted assurances of sober be-haviour. The tale goes on with a momentary parody of sanctimony:

[1] R. F. Brinkley (ed.), *Coleridge on the Seventeenth Century* (1955), pp. 519–20.

But since thou like a contrite penitent,
Charitably warn'd of thy sinnes, dost repent
These vanities, and giddinesses, loe
I shut my chamber doore, and come, lets goe.
But sooner may a cheape whore, who hath beene
Worne by as many severall men in sinne,
As are black feathers, or musk-colour hose,
Name her childs right true father, 'mongst all those:
Sooner may one guesse, who shall beare away
The Infanta of London, Heire to an India;
And sooner may a gulling weather Spie
By drawing forth heavens Scheme tell certainly
What fashioned hats, or ruffes, or suits next yeare
Our subtile-witted antique youths will weare;
Then thou, when thou depart'st from mee, canst show
Whither, why, when, or with whom thou wouldst go.

The comic exasperation of the speaker is so surely mimed and orchestrated that it perfectly places itself. The satirist's role becomes a part of the satire, its affectation of immunity clearly judged to *be* an affectation.

That affectation, indeed, is an essential part of 'Satyre 1's' subject. When, at the opening, Donne offers himself in the edifying role of devoted-scholar-hard-at-his-books, the mockery is plain – not so much mocking scholarly seclusion as such, as the affectation of it into which he has fallen – hence the lugubrious note:

Away thou fondling motley humorist,
Leave mee, and in this standing wooodden chest,
Consorted with these few bookes, let me lye
In prison, and here be coffin'd, when I dye;
Here are Gods conduits, grave Divines; and here
Natures Secretary, the Philosopher;
And jolly Statesmen, which teach how to tie
The sinewes of a cities mistique bodie;
Here gathering Chroniclers, and by them stand
Giddie fantastique Poëts of each land.
Shall I leave all this constant company,
And follow headlong, wild uncertaine thee?

Shall he? Quite inescapably the answer is, Yes. The infinitely distractable state of his mind has already manifested itself in the way he turns his 'constant' sages into boon companions ('jolly', 'giddie' and 'fantastique'); and even his taste in metaphors, rather low metaphors ('Gods *conduits*, grave Divines', if you please!), indicates that his mind is already out in the streets though he isn't. At the very moment he extols the pleasures of study, his enthusiasm is becoming tinged with contempt. How pleasant to be one of God's conduits. How grand to be one of those omnipotent 'Statesmen'! How 'jolly' indeed! Or to be 'Natures Secretary'! And yet, why waste time on a mere pen-pushing underling, when at one's door lies Nature herself? When the pair finally set out, Donne's alacrity is so marked that he leaves his seducer standing.

The rest of 'Satyre 1' goes on to expose a Donne just as fatally fascinated as the foppish companion who entices him away, with the sordid turbulence of the London streets. Though he treads them with infinitely more circumspection and gravity, a Malvolio in Cheapside, the gravity is simply the crowning incongruity. The pose of Donne's satirical stance – always one of the most difficult literary postures to sustain without pomposity or foolish vehemence – is extremely elegant. But this poise unites him with his audience, by its amused confession of a common fallibility.

The poise makes possible an exquisite little coda (better than the rest of the poem put together) at the end of 'Satyre 4'. For 240-odd lines, Donne has been passionately denouncing that bladder swollen with vanity, the Court, when he is suddenly overtaken by a hot flush of modest sanctimony. 'I am not worthy,' he cries, covered with confusion:

> Preachers which are
> Seas of Wit and Arts, you can, then dare,
> Drowne the sinnes of this place, for, for mee
> Which am but a scarce brooke, it enough shall bee
> To wash the staines away; Although I yet
> With *Macchabees* modestie, the knowne merit
> Of my worke lessen: yet some wise man shall,
> I hope, esteeme my writs Canonicall.

The tongue moves with visible relish around the inside of the cheek, ending on the quizzical mockery of that unmistakably interrogative 'Canonicall'.

There is a sureness of touch here, and a humanity for lack of which even so great a satirist as Pope fell sometimes into self-righteous rant. Donne of course couldn't sustain it; but he could hit it off wonderfully at times. And he remained salutarily aware that being a satirist had dangerous affinities with being a fop – the fop whose voice we hear exquisitely mimicked at the opening of 'Satyre 2':

> Sir; though (I thanke God for it) I do hate
> Perfectly all this towne, yet there's one state...

That, in the incisive and devastating judgment it makes, and makes with complete implicitness, is worth pages of Restoration comedy.

Participatory satire though. It isn't a pharisaical process of drawing back the skirts and stepping high across the foul place; it is one of reckless participation.

We came to these poems by way of a philosophy of wit, and the poems themselves grow out of some such philosophy. One could perhaps summarise it in the proposition that human imagination finds its chief nutriment in the absurdities of the world it inhabits. Yet, by the fanatical proliferation of startling and insane comparisons, Wit asserts its sovereignty over even that chaotic external world, exulting in its own agility. In the portrait of the playwright ('Satyre 2') for instance, the exultation strikes me as much more important than the animus:

> One, (like a wretch, which at Barre judg'd as dead,
> Yet prompts him which stands next, and cannot reade,
> And saves his life) gives ideot actors meanes
> (Starving himselfe) to live by his labor'd sceanes;
> As in some Organ, Puppits dance above
> And bellows pant below, which them do move.

If such an imagination is interested in Order at all, it is interested in it as a perennial human delusion – the trip-wire in Nature's vast practical joke at the expense of hopeful, tidy-minded humanity. In reality Nature is a jumble, or like Flavia's face in 'Elegie 2', an anagram which makes mock of our expectations of beauty and proportion. The man of wit, however, expecting nothing *less* than proportion, is free to exult in the disproportion:

> Marry, and love thy *Flavia*, for, shee
> Hath all things, whereby others beautious bee,
> For, though her eyes be small, her mouth is great,

Though they be Ivory, yet her teeth be jeat,
Though they be dimme, yet she is light enough,
And though her harsh haire fall, her skinne is rough;
What though her cheeks be yellow, her hair's red,
Give her thine, and she hath a maydenhead.
These things are beauties elements, where these
Meet in one, that one must, as perfect, please.

. . . .

Though all her parts be not in th'usuall place,
She'hath yet an Anagram of a good face.

It is celebratory poetry – celebrating the disorder by which all
things (and especially poetry) increase. When Donne establishes
witty connexions between the disparate parts of his populous world he
is celebrating simultaneously the infinite variety of nature, which
makes so many things so different from each other, and the gymnastic
triumphs of human intelligence which can confound them in defiance
of nature. The rapacious legal land-shark in 'Satyre 2' is a splendidly
sustained example:

For as a thrifty wench scrapes kitching-stuffe,
And barrelling the droppings, and the snuffe,
Of wasting candles, which in thirty yeare
(Relique-like kept) perchance buyes wedding geare;
Peecemeale he gets lands, and spends as much time
Wringing each Acre, as men pulling prime.
In parchments then, large as his fields, hee drawes
Assurances, bigge, as gloss'd civill lawes,
So huge, that men (in our times forwardnesse)
Are Fathers of the Church for writing lesse.
These hee writes not; nor for these written payes,
Therefore spares no length; as in those first dayes
When Luther was profest, He did desire
Short *Pater nosters*, saying as a Fryer
Each day his beads, but having left those lawes,
Addes to Christs prayer, the Power and glory clause.
But when he sells or changes land, he'impaires
His writings, and (unwatch'd) leaves out, *ses heires*,
As slily as any Commenter goes by
Hard words, or sense; or in Divinity
As controverters, in vouch'd Texts, leave out
Shrewd words, which might against them cleare the doubt.

These innocent/malicious comparisons of course are aimed partly at eternal devious, comfort-loving, egocentric human nature – the same the world over, in kitchen wenches and Protestant reformers, legal foxes and biblical expositors. But the breathless multiplication of unpredictable simile gives us a quite extraordinarily dense and populous world – a kind of milling, intellectual fairground in which all but the most agile are likely to perish in the crush. But the agile Donne, whose plumed hat appears jauntily among the crowds from time to time, not only displays an infectious delight at the immense, thronging mass, but he grows more exuberant as the turmoil grows more confounding. So poet and reader, satirist and audience, collaborate joyfully in the activities of mutual delight and derision, and, like the wise men they are, laugh a great deal.

But the analogy of the party wit-cracker of course implies limitations. To call these poems 'performances' is to indicate that we are dealing with an art which is finally *inventive* rather than *creative*. Inventiveness is of the essence – keeping the balls in the air, the pot on the boil. That's why the improvisatory feel of the rhythms is so important: it's the medium through which we receive the inventive bravura. The danger of a mode, though, which relies so heavily upon invention, is that the juggler of wit will drop one of his coloured balls and become embarrassing in his pretence that nothing has happened. And the longer he goes on the more certain that is to happen. The happiest extrication the performer can expect, really, is some witty pretence that he meant to drop the ball, after which he can throw himself candidly on the audience's goodwill. Satirical activity of this kind, therefore, can have no structure beyond the episodic, and no satisfactory termination except by courtesy of its hearers. The creative shaping which gives a structure an inner necessity of its own is not available to mere inventiveness. Most of the *Satyres* go on too long, and they end more often with a whimper than a bang.

With the *Elegies* the problems are even more acute. We are still at the same party, but something ugly has crept into the social tone. It's as if the performer has gone on too long, attempted a jest or two which have misfired, and has overstrained the bond with his audience. As *their* participating warmth wanes, *he* begins to strut. The wit becomes coarser, and those who consent to remain a part of it find themselves implicated in a defensive pact of the elite against the herd: they are appointed wits in the great world of fools, viz. the great world of those whose backs are visible, walking away from the scene of wit, having begun to find it more than a little tedious. It's in these circumstances that iconoclasm is born as a style of humour – shouts of abuse directed at the retreating backs – and the remaining audience finds itself bearing the brunt of the Wit's ill-temper. Doubling for the departed stuffed shirts, they must agree to be stupefied (in their stolid bourgeois way) by the daring young Donne, and they must suppress, for their own part, any rising suspicion that the daring is really pretty conventional.

As long as the iconoclasm is carried off with style and lightness the fact that there is nobody present who actually worships the 'icons' need not spoil the fun. But when the iconoclast becomes swollen and flushed with the grossness of his own conceits and seems to desire nothing more than to shock and then to snigger (I'm thinking of pieces like 'Elegie 7: The Comparison', or 'Elegie 18: Loves Progress' or 'Elegie 20: Loves Warre') the only appropriate response seems to be to walk away.

A good few of the *Elegies*[1] suffer from this kind of self-advertising cleverness. They don't, by and large, open out in the collaborative way the *Satyres* do. They tend to be very consciously emancipated (i.e. in bondage to their emancipation), and they continually insult their reader by supposing him to be rather adolescently susceptible to shock. Listen, for instance, to Donne ringing the changes on the old sex-as-war metaphor. It cannot work at all unless the reader affects to find the tired old equivoques new and striking – which is exactly what, at this late date in the history of bawdy innuendo, they cannot be:

> Other men war that they their rest may gayne;
> But wee will rest that wee may fight agayne.
> Those warrs the ignorant, these th'experienc'd love,
> There wee are alwayes under, here above.
> There Engins farr off breed a just true feare,
> Neere thrusts, pikes, stabs, yea bullets hurt not here.
>
> ('Elegie 20: Loves Warre')

The metaphors are strictly *not used*: to register the slick antitheses is

---

1 Five of the *Elegies* given by Grierson are unlikely to be by Donne. They are 'Elegies 12–15' and 'Elegie 17'. The matter is debated by Helen Gardner, in her edition.

to dispose of the images; they perish once the point is made. And yet they are revealing enough if one does pause over them. Particularly revealing it is, that, at the very moment the poet is congratulating himself fatuously upon being 'experienc'd', he should betray a totally unrecognised fear, almost horror, of sexuality ('thrusts, pikes, stabs'), so that one is left wondering whether he chose the war metaphor, or it chose him. Fear and aggression and coarseness of sentiment proffer themselves as a fierce challenge to the queasy sensibilities of squeamish readers. But the reader who is not himself squeamish, and who requires no such symbolic liberation through the frightened reactions of others, sees only...fear, aggression, and coarseness of sentiment. One doesn't need to invoke the shade of Ovid to understand the phenomenon: one simply has to have an eye for the perennially Ovidian in human behaviour. It's a strain which carries over into too many of the Songs and Sonets.

The same bondage to cheap kinds of emancipation marks 'Elegie 3: Change'. Donne wants to be admired for his libertarian ethics, yet any perceptive reader can discern so much more there than the cynical panache. It winds up resoundingly enough:

> Change'is the nursery
> Of musicke, joy, life, and eternity.

It might be 'A Defence of Womens Inconstancy' all over again, but it isn't. The poem is shot through with incompatible worries and aggressions, and the 'argument', if one bothers to follow it through, is self-refuting. Far from having earned the right to celebrate Change with the serene beatitude of those lines, Donne, countermined by his logic, betrayed by his analogies (why are waters 'more putrifi'd' in the sea than elsewhere?), and subverted by the quaver in his voice ('yet much, much I feare thee'), is in complete disarray. He appears, however, to be either so besotted with the bravado of his pre-selected role, or so superficially engaged in the undertaking altogether, as to be unaware of it.

Some of the more dramatic, and Ovidian, pieces, like 'Elegie 4: The Perfume', can be lively in proportion as they succeed in creating the emancipated young man dramatically within the poem, giving him to us with a fulness that is open to comic judgment. But for so sophisticated a courtier, Donne's humour has a surprising schoolboy bathos when he can even descend to jokes about smelly feet, and the throwaway ending of 'The Perfume' indicates how little he cares about the enterprise anyway.

Struggling among the coils of this rather dated and fashionable verse-making (dated because fashionable) are a few half-strangled moments of sombre, almost gloomy earnestness. 'Elegie 5: His Picture' is the only piece which sustains that tone for the length of a whole poem. But even when the poem breaks up into interesting fragments and the sombre is jumbled with the pert and perky, something persuasively sober in the voice detains one momentarily, as in the grave, ebbing cadences which close 'Elegie 9: The Autumnall':

> Since such loves naturall lation is, may still
>   My love descend, and journey downe the hill,
> Not panting after growing beauties, so,
>   I shall ebbe out with them, who home-ward goe.

'Elegie 16: On his Mistris' excites the same kind of attentive expectancy, and it's very disconcerting, as one gets further into the poem, to find Donne permitting himself – or is it another creature escaped from his menagerie of personae? – a xenophobic diatribe against the diseased French, the spongy Dutch, and other deviant national groups who can't quite manage to be English. Disconcerting because the opening seemed to promise much more:

> By our first strange and fatall interview,
> By all desires which thereof did ensue,
> By our long starving hopes, by that remorse
> Which my words masculine perswasive force
> Begot in thee, and by the memory
> Of hurts, which spies and rivals threatned me,
> I calmly beg...

You can hear the intent stillness, the charged atmosphere of the opening – love felt as in itself a mysterious and awesome thing – being flawed by loud literary conventionalities like those Ovidian 'spies and rivals'. The combination of Roman elegy as his model, and the particular English audience he seems to have presupposed for his imitations – an exclusively male elite, which, though it prided itself on knowing the world, also took itself to *be* the only world that mattered – these factors pushed Donne's wit too far in the direction of display

for any wholly tactful handling of the love reality to be possible. We
are thrust back into the world of Lovelace.

Tact of that difficult kind is, nevertheless, what the 'Elegie' very
nearly recovers at the end:

> When I am gone, dreame me some happinesse,
> Nor let thy lookes our long hid love confesse,
> Nor praise, nor dispraise me, nor blesse nor curse
> Openly loves force, nor in bed fright thy Nurse
> With midnight startings, crying out, oh, oh,
> Nurse, ô my love is slaine, I saw him goe
> O'r the white Alpes alone; I saw him I,
> Assail'd, fight, taken, stabb'd, bleed, fall, and die.
> Augure me better chance, except dread *Jove*
> Thinke it enough for me to'have had thy love.

It's not an accident that one catches echoes here, in sentiment and
cadence, of the 'Song: Sweetest love, I doe not goe'; and when critics
insist, on scanty evidence, that this *Elegie* at least must have been
addressed to Ann More, they are paying a naively misplaced tribute
to that special kind of authenticity which makes Donne a great poet.
Unaffected tenderness like this is one of the hardest things in poetry
to achieve. It always tends to melt on contact with the outer air. The
miraculous ingredient which prevents that here – that extraordinary
smile of tender scepticism – is uniquely Donne's own. But to smile it,
even to himself, Donne has to move right outside the world in which
most of the *Elegies* were composed. The performance ends. The
audience disperses. The voice takes on the difficult candour which is
required to address the one person you cannot hope to fool.

3

'Ingenious absurdity' and the 'more noble and more adequate conception'
Songs and Sonets I

Donne's early writing makes one unfailing demand on its readers: agility. We have to be awake to the endless self-betrayals the tone can surprise us into; and we must be very limber to handle those perversions of logic so flagrant that the guffaw dies in the throat, or to avoid falling for the affectations of blunt good sense which rapidly reveal themselves to be intellectual booby-traps. Least of all is Donne to be trusted when he puts on his 'sincere' voice. One recalls Falstaff's comment on Mistress Quickly: 'A man knows not where to have her.' In the early verse, the quicksilver quality calls for a kind of intellectual athleticism. In the great lyrics this has been refined into something infinitely subtler. The poetry demands a sensitivity to every nuance of the voice and every shadow of expression that crosses the face. Treacherousness of tone has become fineness of emotional discrimination.

As we move on to the *Songs and Sonets*, I shall be recalling fairly often both the treacherousness and the fineness, and it may be worth dwelling a little on the reasons for the insistence. They are, first, because failure to reckon with it has led to a systematic overrating of some of Donne's most treacherous pieces – 'The Canonization' being one. Again, it has led to readings of others which are naive to the point of crudity – things like that not uncommon version of 'The Sunne Rising' which sees it as a glorious and irresponsible immersion in the Eternal Present of erotic self-surrender (a poem which might have been written by Browning, but by Donne, never).

But the slipperiness of tone also needs to be kept before our eyes, because we're still bedevilled by critics who are altogether too prompt to pronounce on 'Donne's neo-platonism', or 'Donne's philosophy of love', or 'Donne's faith', without ever enquiring in what sense they are Donne's at all, or how he might be conceived to be holding them. Which Donne, anyway? one might profitably ask – especially of the neo-platonisers. Even when he does speak, and can be shown to speak, *in propria persona*, that is as often to be translated 'in his own *persona*', as 'in his own person'. When thou hast Donne, thou hast not Donne, for he has more – that profoundly serious 'Hymne' is partly a recognition, in deathly surroundings, that his congenital addiction to irony has imprisoned him in a barren limbo of involuntary impassivity, fear of relationship (relationship even with God – and again the comparison with Eliot urges itself), and perpetual defensive role-playing. Though I have argued that the term 'persona', as it applies to Donne, is a critically two-edged weapon, there is no doubt at all that it does very often apply.

The *Divine Poems* themselves raise the matter of Donne's tonal subtlety from another angle: because there, and especially in the *Holy Sonnets*, the subtlety is partially in abeyance. That lithe self-awareness which had perceived a larger ironic context for every attitude adopted, and which had scented the incipiently ridiculous long before it had come into view, seems somehow to have been contravened. So much so, that the reader who has sharpened his wits on the *Satyres* and the love lyrics may find he has to take the edge off them again, before he can entirely relish the *Holy Sonnets*. It's as if Donne's movement into belief involved quieting the restless faculty of self-parody. The heart which had loved to be 'subtile to plague itselfe', as 'The Blossome' puts it, now sets itself a task of rigorous simplification – the task called devotion; and attitudes which could never have passed unscrutinised in earlier days, flaunt themselves in gaudy pulpit rhetoric and enter unchallenged. If, as seems likely, most of the *Sonnets* are contemporaneous with the later *Songs and Sonets*, that makes the disjunction between religious and secular vision all the more striking. That Donne should have relinquished one of his most characteristic poetic resources as he stood on the threshold of the priesthood, is a fact that cries out for comment – especially since the relinquishment was never complete, as my allusion to 'A Hymne to God the Father' has just made plain.

Most importantly, though, one needs to cultivate agility and flexibility because there are a number of Donne's most consummate things which are only fully available to the reader who will enter into the infinitely delicate play of tonal ironies across the 'statements' to which the poem commits itself. One thinks of that wonderful achievement of high civilisation, 'Aire and Angels' ('high' in the truest sense, not achieving its elevation by an affected contempt for the simpler human realities). Unless we see the pits and snares which that beautiful urbanity is sidestepping, unless we sense the presence of continual subtle temptations to stray from the perfect tact and perfect magnanimity of manner which the poem achieves, we shall have missed the poem. That is true, I think, of all Donne's finest things.

But in the *Songs and Sonets* we find another by-product of Donne's persistent role-playing: a series of poems where he succeeds in isolating one of his roles, breaking it off, as it were, from the main mass of his preoccupations, and giving it a poem to develop itself in. The element of role, in the *Elegies* for instance, had often been a perplexity to the reader, who kept hearing, in disconcerting antiphony, the voice of Ovid and the voice of Donne. Now, by a finer dramatic instinct, Donne has transmuted the uneasy personae of the *Elegies* into a fully realised dramatic speaker. Role no longer perplexes; it is both explicit and enjoyed – enjoyed partly, I suspect, for the relative simplicity of feeling it permits Donne (limpid solutions of hate, or contempt, or flippancy, not the turbid compounds one finds elsewhere). The comparative relaxation is obvious in the easy loquacity of poems of amorous 'cynicism' like 'The Indifferent', 'Communitie' or 'Confined Love' and the many similar exercises in dramatic or lyric monologue. 'The Apparition' and 'Womans Constancy' are two of the most perfectly turned of these.

It's not a coincidence, though, that one uses terms like 'turned', 'poised', 'finished', to describe the achievement. The poems, with their self-approving air of being finished off, consummated, have a closed feeling about them. They're so conspicuously well-made that you're immediately involved in talking about form and art, the handling of the stanza, the brilliant mimesis of the speaking voice, in short, the craft. Whereas the greatest art doesn't, I think, suggest such categories – or not so promptly. Donne's mastery here is achieved by excluding all-that-is-not-art from the small circle of the poem. It isn't the greater mastery which forms imaginative wholes with a

plenitude, an amplitude so palpable that you have consciously to
remind yourself of the things that have been left out. And it's with
that qualification that we must take the 'unity of tone' for which the
poems are often admired: the unity is achieved by suppressing whole
expressive registers of the human speaking voice. An example to test
my generalities upon:

> Now thou hast lov'd me one whole day,
> To morrow when thou leav'st, what wilt thou say?
> Wilt thou then Antedate some new made vow?
>   Or say that now
> We are not just those persons, which we were?
> Or, that oathes made in reverentiall feare
> Of Love, and his wrath, any may forsweare?
> Or, as true deaths, true maryages untie,
> So lovers contracts, images of those,
> Binde but till sleep, deaths image, them unloose?
>   Or, your owne end to Justifie,
> For having purpos'd change, and falsehood; you
> Can have no way but falsehood to be true?
> Vaine lunatique, against these scapes I could
>   Dispute, and conquer, if I would,
>   Which I abstaine to doe,
> For by to morrow, I may thinke so too.
>
> ('Womans Constancy')

The persona so elegantly sustained throughout, here, is not so
much an instrument of self-exploration, as a self-subsistent *device* in the
poem. The poem, accordingly, makes – indeed, envisages – no progress
in its investigations. You may retort that poetry need not be an
investigation of anything, and 'Womans Constancy' lies ready to
hand to prove your point. But one may also enquire, in turn, what
poetry has to offer beyond an inspired mimicry if it dispenses with the
exploratory, if there is no self behind the mask. To put the general
question in specific terms: why do we not read the last line of 'Womans
Constancy' as a devastating comment on the speaker of the poem:
'For by tomorrow, I may think *so*, too'? I.e. within a day, like the
whore he addresses, he too will be fabricating excuses, thinking *so* too,
being true to his innate falsehood, and vainly lunatic in the defence of
his compulsive promiscuity? '*So*' can mean all of these things. Yet

the poem's commitments to flamboyancy of gesture are so heavy that the possibility does not become operative as anything more than a vague amusement. Donne has put such a fine finish on his artefact that one cannot get through to the psychological or moral reality it figures. The not getting through, of course, is in itself a kind of pleasure – 'After all, there is but one Donne.' was Coleridge's admiring comment on this piece. If I can't entirely share his admiration, it is only because I believe there is more than one Donne.

The perfectly finished work comes dangerously close to being the dead work. To put the case in extreme form – even so brilliant a piece as 'The Apparition', for all its controlled drama of a hissing, impotent venom, still exists in a kind of human void, unconnected: a portent, not an experience. The short, uneasy laugh it extorts from us, as our tribute of admiration for Donne's virtuosity, is uneasy because there can be no plotting this strange parabola of feeling on any of the available human graphs. That is the poem's unique achievement; also, its drastic limitation. For isn't this another case where imagination has failed to reach that heat and incandescence where the poem and its referent in the world of experience fuse with each other – the moment when invention becomes creation, and persona becomes self.

Nevertheless the persona, the mask, can come strikingly into its own. It happens when the mask is something the poet would do without if he could, but the poem gives us the conditions which make it indispensable to him. The Donne of 'A Feaver' is in that predicament. He starts from a position of quite ludicrous self-consciousness: he wants to send a get-well message, which is in itself an absurd thing to do, and he is in absurd agonies lest he appear to be too serious about it. The only outlet for his feelings seems to lie in logical slapstick and verbal buffoonery:

> Oh doe not die, for I shall hate
> All women so, when thou art gone,
> That thee I shall not celebrate,
> When I remember, thou wast one.

There would seem to be no hope that this contorted mind will ever find a way through the thickets of its congenital self-derision. It will clown itself into silence. Yet within two more lines, the pressure of

48

something forcing up *through* the self-derision has generated an hyperbole of quite astonishing power:

> But when thou from this world wilt goe,
> The whole world vapors with thy breath.

And at the end of the poem the hyperbole itself has become a vehicle for what one now recognises to have been an exorbitance of feeling, not an extravagance of manner. The feeling still requires that protective shell of exaggeration, but the tone is sober, grave, *sostenuto*. Donne has fought his way through to candour:

> Yet t'was of my minde, seising thee,
> Though it in thee cannot persever.
> For I had rather owner bee
> Of thee one houre, than all else ever.

The mask is now a matter of tact – Donne not wishing to expose the woman to an intrusive emotion she may not choose to entertain or reciprocate – and it permits us access to the genuine emotion which can feel the *need* of such tact. The mask is no longer worn for disguise or evasion.

At other times, the hard, bright, gem-like immunity of the persona splits open to reveal a richer iridescence and a richer human ambiguity within. Such poems are, of course, much less satisfactory as art; the tones are imperfectly integrated and there are occasional ugly cracks in the voice which, while they may be dramatising coarseness of sentiment, seem also to have been overtaken by the coarseness. Like the conclusion of 'Loves Alchymie':

> Hope not for minde in women; at their best
> Sweetnesse and wit, they'are but *Mummy*, possest.

But the voice, even in its harshnesses, speaks out of a real world of pain and constriction, mad aspiration and ashy disillusion, as the voice of 'Womans Constancy' did not.

> Some that have deeper digg'd loves Myne then I,
> Say, where his centrique happinesse doth lie:
> I have lov'd, and got, and told,
> But should I love, get, tell, till I were old,
> I should not finde that hidden mysterie;
> Oh, 'tis imposture all...

Role is opening the way to utterance.

All these contradictory manifestations of wit are to be found in 'The Canonization' – the self-exploratory role-playing and the swaggering behind a defensive mask; the perfection of art bordering upon human nullity; the treacherous manipulation of irony and the spectacle of the ironist self-betrayed. It's a central poem for the understanding of Donne, in that the critical weight one is prepared to give it in Donne's output determines the way one will read the rest. It seems to me that if we take 'The Canonization' as the highest reach of his wit or as a classic statement of his doctrine of love, we shall put both the highest reaches and the classic statements permanently out of reach.

The opening seems entirely in the zestful spirit of the *Satyres*, with its startling mobility of expression, the sly smirk wiped off the moment it is detected, the careless affectation of sturdy, indeed stolid, common-sense housing a murderously-whetted blade of malice.

> For Godsake hold your tongue, and let me love,
>   Or chide my palsie, or my gout,
>   My five gray haires, or ruin'd fortune flout,

(two calamities of equal magnitude, given my palsied need to simulate eternal youth)

>   With wealth your state, your minde with Arts improve,

(two analogous processes: the arithmetic application of an additional commodity...which says something about the quality of 'your minde')

>   Take you a course, get you a place,
>   Observe his honour, or

(if honour is too high a reach for your wit, too disinterested a contemplation)

>   his grace,

(which may do you some good)

>   Or the Kings reall, or his stamped face
>   Contemplate,

(contemplations which are properly conjoined, since both are tainted
with cupidity)

> what you will, approve,
> So you will let me love.

The basic strategy is now clear: a disarming confession of practical
incompetence laid as a bait to bloat and poison the practical and the
competent who are vain enough to snap it up. But the resourcefulness
of the development surpasses expectation, in its gleeful pumping up
of stock poetic hyperbole until it bursts under the strain:

> Alas, alas, who's injur'd by my love?
> What merchants ships have my sighs drown'd?
> Who saies my teares have overflow'd his ground?
> When did my colds a forward spring remove?
> When did the heats which my veines fill
> Adde one more to the plaguie Bill?

The mockery is two-edged in its acute self-awareness: the practical-
minded friend may be absurd in his fears that the normal world will
somehow be disrupted; that world is as immortal as human vicious-
ness:

> Soldiers finde warres, and Lawyers finde out still
> Litigious men, which quarrels move,
> Though she and I do love.

But the lover is also absurd who will exaggerate his sighs and tears,
his freezings and fryings. They're no such great matters as he will
have us believe. The cosmic hyperbole dresses up a very simple fact:
'she and I do love'. So far everything is beautifully under control. The
slightly idiot harmlessness of the lovers nicely balances the more-than-
slightly menacing features of The Practical Life, so that the speaker,
aware of both, is committed to neither. Despite the quicksilver
evasiveness, there is nevertheless a solidity and assurance of tone (one
voice not many) which convinces us of the masterful presence, the
controlling intelligence.

But now follows the stanza discussed in the first chapter ('Call us
what you will, wee are made such by love...'). The voice suddenly
becomes dry, pedantical and defensive; the drastic impropriety of the
theological conceits throws the reader into confusion, and Donne

retreats into an ironic smokescreen of quite remarkable density. It's all highly entertaining and faintly unsatisfactory.

I shan't argue that unsatisfactoriness at length; those who care to read volumes on the subject are already well supplied. In any case, with so complex and accomplished a poem, where even the uncertainties of feeling are elegantly wrought, commentary tends to become less conclusive the more it aspires to exhaustiveness. So let me simply put the case, and let it lie. In dealing with his dramatically implied critic (in the first two stanzas) Donne is robust and vigorous. But at Stanza 3, the implied presence evaporates and we get both a thinning out of wit and a new note of introspective musing. Significantly, the 'she' of 'she and I do love' gets wholly subsumed into the synthetic 'wee' which is the subject of the subsequent apologetics.

Now that the enquiring friend *has* held his tongue, Donne, deprived of that convenient sounding board, seems not to know quite what he thinks. The aspersions so indignantly repelled before, now begin to take hold of him. Is this love, too, absurd? No answer. Instead we're given, with something very much akin to levity, traditional erotic emblems of futility (moth and candle, the burning taper), fragments of alchemical and bestiary lore, snippets of neo-platonic theorising oddly emptied of all emotive content ('So to one *neutrall* thing both sexes fit'); and finally the proclamation of their 'Mysterious' status, from which the canonization conceit develops in the rest of the poem. But that conceit entails an inflation of sentiment just as grandiose as the Petrarchan hyperboles Donne has already punctured – the sigh/gales, the tear/floods and the passion/fevers. Inevitably we take the canonization as existing on the same level of factitiousness.

Now the poem might very well develop from this point. But the self-consciousness so splendidly exploited in the first two stanzas is beginning to eat out the heart of the poem. It's possible, of course, to trace a discursive logic in this train of emblems; but what concerns me is the disappearance of any felt *content* for that logic. And the clue to this unexpected attenuation of feeling is located somewhere close beside that hyperconscious punning on 'dye' (repeated, you'll notice, in Stanza 4). It's utterly unclear whether the faintly derisive note here is directed at the love, or at the notion of a 'mystery', or both. Anyway, one is so conscious of the pun *as* pun, that the intended (was it?) identification of copulation and resurrection serves in fact to drive a wedge between the two ideas. The hyperbolic force of the identification may derive from the impropriety of the comparison, but the impropriety points to the impossibility of the identification. Donne appears perfectly aware of this state of affairs; but that merely enhances our perplexity.

The spectacle of wit stumbling from a daring joke into uneasy impropriety is one we shall meet again in Donne – frequently in the context of a theological conceit like this one. The love itself, anyway, to make matters worse, is, we learn in the next stanza, 'unfit for tombes and hearse', i.e. at the very least clandestine, and probably disreputable, though that unfitness simply spurs Donne into new acts of defiance. Yet the niggling uneasiness spreads like a creeping infection to a suspicion of the poetic act itself;

> And if unfit for tombes and hearse
> Our legend bee, it will be fit for verse.

There's something so miscalculated about the contemptuous stress that falls on the word 'verse', yielding so much ground to the practical friend, that Donne is obliged to rehearse the couplet again twice over, before it will come out with the correct intonation:

> And if no peece of Chronicle wee prove,
> We'll build in sonnets pretty roomes.

'Pretty roomes', though, with its quaint, bemused flimsiness, won't do either. Try again:

> As well a well wrought urne becomes
> The greatest ashes, as halfe-acre tombes.

The magnanimity, the manly spaciousness of the opening is very nearly recaptured here. But it's spoiled, just as the recovered poise of the last stanza is spoiled, by the reappearance of that theological conceit with its willed exaggeration of sentiment:

> And by these hymnes, all shall approve
> Us *Canoniz'd* for Love.

They are love's martyrs only in the sense that they have 'died' on the bed of love. Their 'hymnes' which, we note, *precede* their canonization, are used fraudulently to impose upon the faithful, presenting them with a beatified *fait accompli*. This poem itself (as 'sonnet' and 'hymne') is an instrument of the deception. There is no end to the self-reflecting mirrors, because there is no true self to be reflected.

The poem now moves into the last disintegrating stage of its wit, as Donne struts before the ironically postulated congregation of worshippers, in improving attitudes of erotic sanctity. There are, in the last stanza, some entirely serious (if I can risk the word) claims for the transcendent importance of love as epitomising, distilling, concentrating all the disparate elements of life: Donne thus, in a sense, focuses all the perceptions of the outside world given in those first two stanzas in 'the glasses of [their] eyes'. But these moments are framed by the dominant equivocation, the incipient absurdity of worshipping as heavenly what is present in the poem only as a source of perplexity and uncertainty – this profane love which is somehow supposed to be sacred as well.

Donne is of course aware of the absurdity. It completes his self-deprecatory portrait of the poor mad lover, perishing under the scourge of his self-destructive passion ('Wee can dye by it, if not live by love' – and I think there must be some reference here to the current superstition that every act of kind shortened one's span of life by one day), while embracing still the same hopeless delusions of grandeur. But having taken that point, and having relished the whole excursus of wit that goes with it, we're still left with a vacuum where the content of the love ought to be (we get it only through the parodied fervour of the votive prayer – 'You, to whom love was peace, that now is rage' and so on), and with a faint impression of bad taste in the extravagant final gesture,

> Beg from above
> A patterne of your love!

Intentionally or not (and how could it ever be determined?) coming after the ironic alertness of the rest, this has an unmistakably derisive ring. The self-consciousness has gone into that fatal spiral I mentioned earlier – as if Donne were jeering at anyone who could use such words without irony, and at himself for half attempting it.

As far as I can discover, it's not uncommon to come away from 'The Canonization' with a feeling of distaste. But it's the *why* of that distaste that concerns me. It seems connected somehow with a feeling that the complexities of response in which Donne is dealing are self-indulgent, wanton, factitious – as if there were some invisible but decisive threshold which the poem crosses, after which the habit of irony changes its nature and becomes a *game* in dubious taste. Once that threshold is crossed, the poem dissipates itself. The irony becomes *dis*integrative.

But let me insist…the habit of irony (one could almost call it, in Donne's case, the ironic way of life) is not necessarily like this. It is, I suppose, always 'defeated' in the limited sense that it accepts at the outset the impossibility of pure feelings, or pure motives. But irony, properly, is the acceptance of human experience as essentially communal and open to common interpretations. It is a willingness to have one's feelings observed from many other viewpoints besides one's own, no experience being so wholly private as to be inaccessible to the scrutinies of the disengaged spectator.

In Donne, this ironic critique of subjectivity works usually through self-parody, or mock imposition upon the reader, or through exploratory role-playing – all producing a continually varied play of light across the poetry, as the degree of implied detachment varies from line to line. The whole procedure openly admits the right of the world to scrutinise and censure (Donne after all is constantly doing it himself, to other people's subjectivities, and he cherishes the right sufficiently to make it reciprocal). The intelligent man's duty, as he sees it, is not to repel these criticisms, but to anticipate them as best he may, and to take them up into the continuing processes of his self-knowledge. This is the proper use of irony.

But beyond that indefinable, definite threshold, the operations of irony are reversed. They become an artifice for the assertion of impenetrable subjectivity, the defence-mechanism of a threatened privacy: 'I will say it first, so that you *cannot* say it.' And then the true artistic impersonality mutates into a beleaguered and militant cult of secrecy – a cult of which the writer becomes more the victim than the initiator. Always then, there's the sense of a runaway cart gathering momentum for the inevitable crash. 'The Canonization' is very much like this: a poem that seems to happen by some pretty powerful internal logic, but a logic that one finally deplores. The canonization conceit arises with beguiling naturalness from the investigations of the first two stanzas; but once it has arisen there is no escaping its nemesis, for it brings with it all that uneasy false consciousness that mars other Donne poems besides this one – 'The Extasie' being one salient instance.

I say *false* consciousness, because in both 'The Canonization' and 'The Extasie' the mature awareness of the inevitable scrutinising glances of one's fellow men changes subtly into an immature strutting and posturing before an imagined audience (in the same way as the gay, satiric exuberance of the *Satyres* had degenerated into the self-conscious iconoclasm of the *Elegies*). There's a fundamental similarity of temper between 'The Canonization' and 'The Extasie', which manifests itself in the way both pieces wear their physicality with something of an air, and seem very prone to embark on public apologetics in its behalf. The apologetics involve them in unsettled and unsettling versions of Donne's erotic theology: in 'The Canonization' it was the punning identification of copulation and resurrection; in 'The Extasie', an incarnation joke acts as a kind of nose-ring by which Donne can draw his triumphant synthesis of spiritual and physical round the arena:

> To'our bodies turne wee then, that so
> Weake men on love reveal'd may looke.

As with 'The Canonization', the lover finds it necessary to exhibit himself and his love for the admiration of mankind at large, before he can bring himself to believe in its reality. We 'weake men' are not very edified, I think, especially if we happen to recall Donne in a very different mood, behaving with real delicacy:

> T'were prophanation of our joyes
> To tell the layetie our love.

That kind of love doesn't need an audience to reinforce the sense of its own identity and sanctity. And if there is any doubt about the inde-corum, the unseemliness of the punning notion of love 'reveal'd', in 'The Extasie', it is dispelled by the ending, where the hypothetical 'third party' (this poem's equivalent for the phantom votaries in 'The Canonization'), who has haunted the poem from the beginning, has become an explicit – indeed an invited – voyeur:

> Let him still marke us, he shall see
> Small change, when we'are to bodies gone.

Only guilt could be so insistent that it is not ashamed.

False consciousness. The acute awareness of the judging eyes of the world has shaken Donne loose from his standing. He is unable any longer to possess his experience. Like 'The Canonization', 'The Extasie' is diffracted and diffused into multi-faceted *possible* attitudes, none of which the poem can bring itself to espouse. It is the dispersion of meaning, not its concentration, finally an irresponsibility of imagination.

Yet one wouldn't be without it. Because the ironic way of life, here perverted, represents a serious and adult commitment to the responsibilities of meaning, and its abuse is simply the price one pays for that utterly necessary sense of the corporate penetrability of private experience. When that is lacking, another kind of unseemliness ensues.

I can illustrate it from one of the more confessional of D. H. Lawrence's poems. I choose him because in many ways his approach to matters of love and sexuality is so much more deeply sane than Donne's – there are more than a few documents in the psychopathology of sex to be found in the collected Donne. And yet the unmeditatedly and unguardedly personal in Lawrence's autobiographical love poetry always seems to lack a social dimension and is as a result gauche, uneasy, even (one feels at times) vulgar. Certainly unseemly.

> *First Morning*
> The night was a failure
>   but why not – ?
>
> In the darkness
>   with the pale dawn seething at the window
>   through the black frame
>   I could not be free,
>   not free myself from the past, those others –
>   and our love was a confusion,
>   there was a horror,
>   you recoiled away from me.
>
> Now, in the morning
> As we sit in the sunshine on the seat by the
>   little shrine,
> And look at the mountain-walls,
> Walls of blue shadow,
> And see so near at our feet in the meadow

Myriads of dandelion pappus
Bubbles ravelled in the dark green grass
Held still beneath the sunshine –
It is enough, you are near –
The mountains are balanced,
The dandelion seeds stay half-submerged in
    the grass;
You and I together
We hold them proud and blithe
On our love.
They stand upright on our love,
Everything starts from us,
We are the source.

Certainly a mature love must reckon with 'the past, those others' ('which I desir'd, and got', as Donne has it); and, certainly, if the night was a failure, it will hardly contribute to the poetic truth to pretend otherwise. There is a rightness and a courage about Lawrence's confessional simplicity. But it is not – cannot be – artless. After all, artless candour does not deliberately invite us in on the lovers' colloquy (a poem *is* such an invitation) and then behave as if we had no more rights upon the offered experience than so many attendant dandelions – behave, indeed, as if we weren't there at all. Lawrence turns his back grimly upon one kind of self-consciousness only to fall into another more insidious kind: the kind that self-consciously affects to have left all self-consciousness behind. There is no escaping the entailments of consciousness that way; by clapping the telescope to one's blind eye. If the truth of intimate speech is not to become just another attitude that a poet may strike, the incontrovertible presence of the human world outside the love must be recognised. The recognition would have to be ironic: a recognition that the man who remarks, without a tremor of irony, 'Everything starts from us,/ We are the source' has not only *risked* the mockery of the knowing world: he has *earned* it.

If this seems rather hard on Lawrence, it is worth pondering Donne's fine and tactful handling of an almost identical situation:

The Good-Morrow

I wonder by my troth, what thou, and I
Did, till we lov'd? were we not wean'd till then?

But suck'd on countrey pleasures, childishly?
Or snorted we in the seaven sleepers den?
T'was so; But this, all pleasures fancies bee
If ever any beauty I did see,
Which I desir'd, and got, t'was but a dreame of thee.

And now good morrow to our waking soules,
Which watch not one another out of feare;
For love, all love of other sights controules,
And makes one little roome, an every where.
Let sea-discoverers to new worlds have gone,
Let Maps to other, worlds on worlds have showne,
Let us possesse one world, each hath one, and is one.

My face in thine eye, thine in mine appeares,
And true plaine hearts doe in the faces rest,
Where can we finde two better hemispheares
Without sharpe North, without declining West?
What ever dyes, was not mixt equally;
If our two loves be one, or, thou and I
Love so alike, that none doe slacken, none can die.

Lawrence's miscalculation of tone involved, among other things, a confusion between self-exposure and candour. Donne's great distinction here is to open up a new range of meanings for a word like 'candour' – which, for a congenital ironist, is quite an achievement. They are meanings, furthermore, which illuminate the essential kinship between candour and truth.

4

'Natural and new . . . though not obvious . . . just' –
Songs and Sonets II

I have been evincing, so far, a rather graceless negativity about the *Songs and Sonets*, and the 'case against' a poem never wholly satisfies – not even its propounder. Yet it is necessary, if one is to take Johnson's canons as seriously as they deserve, to admit that a poem like 'The Canonization' is not, in the richest senses of those words, 'natural', 'just' and 'true'; only by that admission can one free oneself to respond to the power of the poems that are. The negative case against Donne is only the shadow cast by a great light – the light radiating from a handful of superb lyrics. By 'light' I mean such bright energy, such piercing purity of feeling as one finds in 'The Good-Morrow', 'The Sunne Rising', 'The Anniversarie', 'A Valediction: forbidding Mourning', 'Sweetest love, I do not goe', 'Aire and Angels', 'Loves Growth'. In the name of poetry of this order, one can afford to be a little brusque with the merely excellent.

And then one pauses over the list; for a moment it looks as if the principle on which it is compiled might be a simple sentimentality about the nature of love. They are all poems of *fulfilled* love. I can resist this damaging inference in two ways: by adding 'Twicknam Garden' (which one tends not to think of as a characteristic Donne love-poem, though it is a very fine one) and that unclassifiable meditative lament and celebratory elegy, 'A Nocturnall upon S. Lucies day' – in some ways an even more impressive poem than any of the others. But if one considers the other great poets of human love in the language, it becomes clearer *why* one doesn't think of this sombre Donne, as *the* Donne: with Chaucer, Wyatt, Marlowe, Shakespeare, Wordsworth, Hardy, it is love in separation and bereavement, or love unconsummated, tainted with despair, that claims the most serious attention; 'Twicknam Garden' and the 'Nocturnall' might pass unnoticed in that assembly. But it is Donne's almost unchallenged distinction to have made poetry out of the exultant, or the more sober mutuality which is what love is usually taken to be about. The exceptions tend only to strengthen the argument: one believes in Spenser's domestic felicity, but one would not want to compare it, in intensity or splendour, with Donne's love; Burns is at his most memorable and gripping in absence, or at parting; the nineteenth-century poets, though they attempt the celebration of love, seem never able to mobilise their full poetic resources behind an undertaking that has come to seem so precious and personal that one can't talk about it in an ordinary voice or ordinary language; or else, like Byron, they talk about it in such ordinary language that it ceases to be either precious or personal. And if we turn to our own times, there is either Yeats' problematical anguish, or the poignant glimpses and powerful incompletions from which Eliot's natural development carries him steadily away. Donne's is the rare case of a love-poet whose main creative impetus ran to affirmation, and the celebratory love poems constitute a unique contribution to the English tradition; they offer something to our understanding of love which is not available elsewhere.

All the same, the sentimentality, which merely ministers to a gratifying conviction that one is already in possession of the meaning of love, and which engages an obliging Donne to confirm one in that happy rightness, is always near enough at hand to call for vigilance. One particularly insidious form of it is the piece of respectability which equates Donne's maturity with his marriage, and goes to extraordinary lengths of scholarly speciousness to suggest that all the best lyrics were addressed to Ann More. It has, at best, the status of myth. Very few of the *Songs and Sonets* can be dated, and one that can be shown to be written after the marriage, 'The Sunne Rising', sounds oddly unlike the bedroom colloquy of a couple several years married. But the dispute is foolish. Once again the 'life' which communicates itself *in* the verse is being referred to a life *outside* the verse for validation – when the 'validation' can only have the effect of coarsening the texture and blurring the outline of an unreproduceable emotional-poetic figure. That we should be tempted to make the reference outward is a tribute to the poetic truth of the representation; but we pay a more meaningful tribute by resisting the impulse and resting in the wholeness of what Donne has given us, and could not have given us in any other way.

So much by way of easy triumphing over popular fallacies. But what is one to say oneself to delineate this central achievement of Donne's? There is a telling episode in *Anna Karenina*, where Tolstoy finds occasion to dramatise the encounter between two antithetical versions of the 'creative', between, in the particular instance, a dauber and a genuine painter. The passage has been used before for expository purposes, but that is only because it puts some essential matters extremely well.

Vronsky and Anna have encountered in Italy the expatriate Russian painter Mikhailov. Vronsky and his friend Golenischev feel free to patronise the painter, on the grounds of his sad deficiency of 'culture', though they're prepared to grant him 'technique' and 'talent'. Vronsky has been daubing away at a portrait of Anna without much success or satisfaction – due, he consoles himself with believing, to his lack of 'technique'. Now he engages Mikhailov to paint Anna's portrait.

From the fifth sitting the portrait impressed everyone, especially Vronsky, not only by its likeness, but by its characteristic beauty. It was strange how Mikhailov could have discovered her special beauty. 'One needs to know and love her as I have loved her to discover the very sweetest expression of her soul,' Vronsky thought, though it was only from this portrait that he had himself learned this sweetest expression of her soul. But the expression was so true that he, and others too, thought they had long known it.

'I have been struggling on forever without doing anything,' he said of his own portrait of her, 'and he just looked and painted it. That's where technique comes in.'[1]

It has, of course, nothing to do with technique – or not in that contemptuous sense – any more than Donne's discovery of the 'special beauty' in fulfilled love has. We're inclined to react that way because we imagine we have 'long known it', and thus we postulate a process of expression which is simply the technical rendering of a known reality. But that just shows how deep the truth of the expression really is. Without the artist we should never have known it, and we

[1] Part 5, ch. 13, tr. Constance Garnett.

continue to know it partly on condition that we return periodically to
see what it was. Nor is it simply a matter of looking and painting
what is seen, looking in one's heart and writing. Mikhailov's qualifica-
tion for the task – as the rest of the episode shows – is a fineness of
human feeling and a sensitivity of response which makes Anna's
'characteristic beauty' available to him as it never is to the coarser-
grained Vronsky.

There's another respect, too, in which the portrait-painting
analogy is a helpful one: the portraitist deals in 'likeness'. The means
he chooses to reach the inner realities is the common outward reality
which is open to all observers. (Perhaps the two realities are one,
anyway.) Donne's finest love poetry is like that, in that it reaches
back into the sensations and the metaphors which have been the
common stock of lovers in all ages – the sensation, for instance, that
one is awakening from a long drugged sleep into a clarity and fresh-
ness of vision never dreamt of before ('And now good-morrow to our
waking soules' – the conception is central and normative in the
deepest sense); the conviction that the eyes of the woman into which
one gazes do not only symbolise, but contain a depth of meaning, and
open on to a reality not to be reached otherwise; the feeling of physical
bounty and profusion containing riches so inexhaustible that wealth
beyond the dreams of avarice can only be a pallid metaphor for them;
the sense of a miraculous exemption from time and all its entangle-
ments – all these things are so familiar we think we have always known
them; and their power in Donne is partly due to the sense in which
we always *have*. And yet if we want to recall what it *is* that we have
known, it is to Donne that we turn. There is the familiar face of the
known experience, but at the same time the translucency, the lumi-
nosity of the inner flame that lights up the familiar face in mysterious
ways.

Donne's artist's eye, though, isn't merely a divine endowment. It
has to be cultivated and disciplined. It grows out of an awareness of
all the multilateral claims of the human situation and the attempt to
weigh them in the most scrupulous scales. That's why I've been
using words like 'tact' and 'truth' to describe Donne's superiority, as
a poet, to Lawrence. He is so much more alive to the multiplicity of
demands that must be satisfied before any expression can be just.
And he wrestles with the consequent problems.

One of the things he must wrestle with is the promptings (not always very delicate) of an experienced sensuality. It is utterly impossible for him to evade comment on his past loves; and yet the mention of them teeters always on the brink of grossness and bravado, or else of a slighting undervaluation of them which is liable to sound too much like the tone of the professional seducer – 'They were all nothing to me. Nothing! It's you I love.' On the other hand, if the acknowledgment of past loves is allowed to degenerate into a disingenuous apology for them, another kind of falseness enters. The meeting and mutuality of man and woman is translated into a dominative mode and what might have been a manly avowal becomes whining and cajoling in timbre.

What seems almost inevitable in such an encounter, though, is the claim for the superiority of this love over all the preceding ones – a claim shot through, necessarily, with contradictions and perplexities. Donne risks the bravado, but he makes it a shared thing:

> I wonder by my troth, what thou, and I
> Did, till we lov'd? were we not wean'd till then?
> But suck'd on countrey pleasures, childishly?
> Or snorted we in the seaven sleepers den?

The experience they share is explicitly sexual: the 'countrey pleasures' are enjoyed between the acres of the rye, 'country matters', in Hamlet's phrase; and the lightly touched suggestions of adolescent enthusiasm combined with practical incompetence (in verbs like 'suck'd' and 'snorted') both admit, and humorously neutralise, the reality of the past. Donne rounds it off with a little whimsical note of self-ratification – 'T'was so' – before he moves on to the dangerous big claim which is the necessary attestation of his good faith: 'But this, all pleasures fancies bee.' The word 'fancies' gets a heavily contemptuous stress, too heavily contemptuous to carry complete conviction, I think. Apart from the meaning (required by the context) of imaginary gratifications, 'fantasies', the word also bears some taint of the amorous 'fancies', young men's fancies, some suggestion of fickleness, which muddies the clear logic of persuasion. The attempt at a soberer reassurance in the remaining lines of the stanza cannot quite escape the muddiness of feeling. All the same, Donne doesn't attempt to dissolve the past totally away with his *post hoc* rationalisings:

> If ever any beauty I did see,
> Which I desir'd, *and got*, t'was but a dreame of thee.

I think it's a mistake to see that tersely parenthetic 'and got' as a piece of aggression. It is the nearest approach to complete candour that the poem has so far made. He is looking her fearlessly in the face and insisting that this too shall be explicit between them; doing so with such force, indeed, that there seems something of the pulled punch, a faintly insulting, soothing, silken note about the rest of the line – 't'was but a dreame of thee'. That inhabits the world of conventional compliment to conventional mistresses. Stanza one thus ends in an unresolved knot, and will remain so as long as the tone remains that of man confronting woman, displaying his maleness and warming to her enjoyment of it.

Instead of tampering with the tone and producing new and uglier complications (as he does in 'The Canonization'), adding new codicils and caveats to an already ambiguous document, Donne simply shakes clear of it all, moves one crucial step nearer to the woman, and the miracle is performed – the lucid, utterly candid note is achieved. The movement now has a joyous, liberated stride about it, which simply walks away from the tangled feelings of Stanza 1 into a new freedom. The world has become wonderfully simple, vast as the new mapmakers could wish, and vaster; but it is at last '*one* world', one 'every where', and that world 'possessed' as the new worlds of the sea-discoverers, or the even huger worlds of the armchair cosmographers, can never be.

> And now good morrow to our waking soules,
> Which watch not one another out of feare;

(the last subsiding wave of that tide of mutual suspicion, which now ebbs back into the great sea that contains it)

> For love, all love of other sights controules,

(the attempt to impose discipline upon the unruly appetite for 'other sights' is replaced by the organic, inward order of love 'controuling')

> And makes one little roome, an every where.
> Let sea-discoverers to new worlds have gone,
> Let Maps to other, worlds on worlds have showne,
> Let us possesse one world, each hath one, and is one.

If you have ever wondered why philosophers, poets and theologians so persistently confound love with a sense of the infinite and an intuition of absolute freedom, the answer is here. That is the 'characteristic beauty' of love, which we have always known, and which Donne makes us know freshly, again.

The stanza is vibrant with the most simple words profoundly touched into life – the '*waking* soules', a phrase which makes the literal awakening after a night of love-making an awakening of the soul's eye as well, an initiation into a new cleansed world of clear vision. Something is rising to consciousness in their eyes as they watch each other, and that something, mysterious, new, and beyond their conscious, willing selves, they can only greet with the simplest salutation available in Elizabethan English: 'Good morrow.' Or the word 'controules'; or the word 'possesse', with its richly physical connotations filled out by contrast with all the other varieties of 'possessing' which are finally dependent on activity, not being – the brief triumph of the explorer, or the more abstract power of the astronomers over worlds they can never enter. All the metaphysical hankerings, all the restless curiosity of intellect which might have squandered itself on these activities is taken up into the single state of 'possessing one world'.

And yet Donne is free, at the same time, to see (and Lawrencean terms are wholly appropriate here) that the possession depends upon the star-like distinctness of the individuals who make up that one world. There is to be no ecstatic merging and mingling, no confounding of pure substance, but oneness, possession, *and* distinctness – 'each hath one, and is one'. Complete clarity of being as well as complete union.

Which gives rise to a metaphor so perfect that it seems not to have been discovered, so much as to have welled up within the poem. We have been aware of that deep mutual gaze, as 'love all love of other sights controules'. But now, as if by some shift into another, beatific, dimension of vision, Donne is able to look more deeply, down *into* their love:

> My face in thine eye, thine in mine appeares.

I hope I won't be misunderstood if I say this is like Dante gazing into the eternal light, as into 'waters clear and tranquil, not so deep that

the bottom is darkened' (*Paradiso*, iii, 11), until he becomes aware of
the spirits who gaze back at him out of that clear fountain; there is
in the Donne image the same faith in the truth which lies *within* the
visible, not behind it. Donne receives his self back again from the
woman, but focused, held, purified in her vision of him. And she like-
wise receives her self back from him. The truth of the 'true plaine
hearts' lies in those *reflected* faces, not in the faces they wear apart
from each other. The deeply satisfied gaze of mutuality has yielded up
its full meaning.

Yet, despite this, the poem moves slowly (and a trifle sadly) away
from that supreme, and supremely natural, moment. It re-enters the
world of more ordinary things, the love of plain and decent people,
where 'true plaine hearts doe in the faces rest'. Perhaps it means that
the true hearts *show* their truth by being content to 'rest' in the truth
the face reveals. But isn't there also a touch of self-depreciation about
the phrase, some awareness that the inevitable return to the ordinary
world of 'true plaine' feeling is a sadness of a kind? Perhaps that is why
Donne ends as he does, turning over the conditions of an impossible
permanency (two hemispheres with neither a West nor a North) with
an urgency and a plangency which, whatever else one says about it, is
not conclusive as a final cadence to *this* poem. He seems to have
established the right to say so much more, and then to have forfeited
it at the last moment.

> What ever dyes, was not mixt equally;
> If our two loves be one, or, thou and I
> Love so alike, that none doe slacken, none can die.

Donne appears to have worked over that last line, but he produced
nothing more satisfactory ('Love just alike in all; none of these loves
can die' was one variant). The conditional construction – conditional
upon impossible stabilities – is a matter which goes deeper than syn-
tax. As a feeling it remains invincible, and it contributes an unexpected
note of earnest pain to the ending.

It feels rather like a situation in which the poet has been forced into
an unreal choice between art and integrity and has opted for integrity.
Almost certainly, though, the unresolved nature of the final stanza
proceeds from the fact that, somewhere in the course of it, Donne
loses the burning awareness of the woman's presence which makes the

first two so potent; and he is left, consequently, with a lapful of doubts and misgivings, trying to piece them together into the required affirmation, and failing. Or perhaps I am wrong, and there was no attempt at affirmation – only the inevitable and eloquent sadness at the passing of a supreme moment.

I think it's helpful to see 'The Good-Morrow' as part of a triptych, with 'The Sunne Rising' at the centre and 'The Anniversarie' flanking it. I am not thinking just of the development (suspiciously neat) in time – 'The Sunne Rising' as a later, more stabilised version of the first morning of 'The Good-Morrow', 'The Anniversarie' looking back after a year – nor of the central image series – discoverers, the mines of the Indies, and the lovers as princes – which runs through the three. I make the suggestion in order to account for a sense that the three together make a statement more comprehensive than any one does singly. They are variants upon a central intuition of fulfilled passion which one ought not to feel obliged to *choose between* – I think that's the feeling.

Be that as it may, in 'The Sunne Rising' the intimacy is at a more developed stage than in 'The Good-Morrow', and the greater geniality of manner reflects a more expansive attitude to the world beyond the lovers. The implicit 'we' of the poem overflows from the 'little roome' to commit acts of usurpation upon 'all States, and all Princes', and there is a recklessness of demeanour which is very different from 'The Good-Morrow''s sober joyousness. The recklessness and the public manner are in fact two qualities that seem to call for comment – if only under the ambiguous heading of 'seriousness'. But I want to do this by fetching something of a circle, and offering for comparison a passage from *The Rainbow* which may help to define the poem's mode more concretely. The passage also has the incidental convenience of filling out my contention that Donne, in treating that lover's sensation of immunity from time, is dealing with a central human experience and doing it in central ways. The poem first:

The Sunne Rising
Busie old foole, unruly Sunne,
Why dost thou thus,
Through windowes, and through curtaines call on us?
Must to thy motions lovers seasons run?

68

Sawcy pedantique wretch, goe chide
Late schoole boyes and sowre prentices,
Goe tell Court-huntsmen, that the King will ride,
Call countrey ants to harvest offices;
Love, all alike, no season knowes, nor clyme,
Nor houres, dayes, moneths, which are the rags of time.

Thy beames, so reverend, and strong
Why shouldst thou thinke?
I could eclipse and cloud them with a winke,
But that I would not lose her sight so long:
If her eyes have not blinded thine,
Looke, and to morrow late, tell mee,
Whether both the'Indias of spice and Myne
Be where thou leftst them, or lie here with mee.
Aske for those Kings whom thou saw'st yesterday,
And thou shalt heare, All here in one bed lay.

She'is all States, and all Princes, I,
Nothing else is.
Princes doe but play us; compar'd to this,
All honor's mimique; All wealth alchimie.
Thou sunne art halfe as happy'as wee,
In that the world's contracted thus;
Thine age askes ease, and since thy duties bee
To warme the world, that's done in warming us.
Shine here to us, and thou art every where;
This bed thy center is, these walls, thy spheare.

The Lawrence comes from the account of the early married love of
Will and Anna Brangwen.

Inside the room was a great steadiness, a core of living eternity. Only far out-
side, at the rim, went on the noise and the destruction. Here at the centre the
great wheel was motionless, centred upon itself. Here was a poised, unflawed
stillness that was beyond time, because it remained the same, inexhaustible,
unchanging, unexhausted.

As they lay close together, complete and beyond the touch of time or
change, it was as if they were at the very centre of all the slow wheeling of
space and the rapid agitation of life, deep, deep inside them all, at the centre
where there is utter radiance, and eternal being, and the silence absorbed in
praise: the steady core of all movements, the unawakened sleep of all wakeful-
ness. They found themselves there, and they lay still, in each other's arms;

for their moment they were at the heart of eternity, whilst time roared far off, for ever far off, towards the rim.

Then gradually they were passed away from the supreme centre, down the circles of praise and joy and gladness, further and further out, towards the noise and the friction. But their hearts had burned and were tempered by the inner reality, they were unalterably glad.

Gradually they began to wake up, the noises outside became more real. They understood and answered the call outside. They counted the strokes of the bell. And when they counted midday, they understood that it was midday, in the world, and for themselves also.

It dawned upon her that she was hungry. She had been getting hungrier for a lifetime. But even yet it was not sufficiently real to rouse her. A long way off she could hear the words, 'I am dying of hunger.' Yet she lay still, separate, at peace, and the words were unuttered. There was still another lapse.

And then, quite calmly, even a little surprised, she was in the present, and was saying:

'I am dying with hunger.'

'So am I,' he said calmly, as if it were of not the slighest significance. And they relapsed into the warm, golden stillness. And the minutes flowed unheeded past the window outside.[1]

The connexions are obvious, because they are profound – not imitation, or influence (Lawrence's reading of Donne was cursory and unenthusiastic), but the tapping of the same deep strata of experience. It's not for nothing, either, that one hears pre-echoes of *Four Quartets* and post-echoes of the Dante Lawrence affected to despise. I assume that we can all see the importance and the magnitude of what Lawrence is undertaking, when I go on to say that he seems to me insufficiently alert to some of the pitfalls. These group themselves around phrases like 'absorbed into reality', or 'the heart of eternity', or 'beyond time'. Partly it's his usual manner of giving us experience from the inside outwards, so that it reaches us refracted and coloured by the consciousness of the two lovers; and they are (the conviction reaches us effortlessly) 'unalterably glad', and will remain so whatever happens subsequently. And yet it's as characteristic of Lawrence's sensibility as it is uncharacteristic of Donne's, that his lovers should be 'passed *away* from the supreme centre, *down*...towards the noise and the friction'. For Donne the experience of being 'beyond time', the

[1] *The Rainbow*, ch. 6.

experience of transcendence, doesn't possess quite the allurement it
has for Lawrence. Actually it's from a heightened *awareness* of 'the
noise and the friction' that 'The Sunne Rising' starts – the awareness
being part of the love. The world of 'late schoole boyes and sowre
prentices' is present to him as something more than 'friction'. He
even registers, by gleefully selecting those two classes of disgruntled
early-risers, the precise time of day out there in 'the world'. Beside
this crisp alertness there's something faintly soporific, drugged about
Will and Anna's happiness.

To put it another way – in their common pursuit of 'reality' in
love, the question, '*Which* reality?' is much more sharply perceived
by Donne, than it is by Lawrence. In some ways it is *the* question that
an absorbed lover must answer (and in fairness to Lawrence, I must
add that my truncated quotation has suppressed his treatment of it).
All the same it's that rather too easy acceptance of one reality as
higher than the other which it is Donne's distinction to avoid. The
overt argument of 'The Sunne Rising' may assert it, but the whole
imaginative movement aims at assimilating the two realities (Love
and The World, roughly speaking) to each other.

Given that it's easier to write a great poem than a great novel every
page of which will stand comparison with a great poem, we may per-
haps let the qualitative comparison lapse. But it does point up Donne's
extreme sensitivity to the solipsistic, egocentric blasphemy against
the *common* reality, which lovers are prone to fall into. He makes it, of
course, makes it extravagantly:

> Thy beams, so reverend, and strong
> Why shouldst thou thinke?
> I could eclipse and cloud them with a winke...

But we're well enough aware who would be left in the dark as a result
of that operation; and Donne lightly stresses the point by a sly drop
in tone:

> But that I would not lose her sight so long...

The careless *superbia* quietly deflates itself: shutting his eyes on the
'reality' represented by the sun, means losing her, or rather, losing
'her sight' – which includes her loving gaze turned upon him, as well
as his vision of her. That rich gift, 'her sight', is received only by

courtesy of the sun, and the whole poem is lit by a particularly warm, golden sun. It may be true that

> Love, all alike, no season knowes, nor clyme,
> Nor houres, dayes, moneths, which are the rags of time;

but love is also (demonstrably) revelling in this very particular moment after sunrise and enhancing its blissful sense of immunity by forming mental images of 'time'. Those images carry such obvious delight to the contemplation of the 'Court-huntsmen' and the 'countrey ants', and the speaker is so plainly in a state of worldly self-possession when he blandly yokes the two together, that the whole issue of ' *Which* reality? is thrown wide open. And at the same time Donne pays his mistress the compliment of bringing his whole nature, in its public and courtly dimensions, as well as its loving and private ones, to do her essential homage.

But there is another obstacle to the celebration of love (which Lawrence by-passed by being a novelist not a poet): it concerns the relationship with the reader entailed by speaking in the first person. It doesn't matter much when one is properly dejected in love. But when one is elated, the possibility that one is simply making an exhibition of an essentially private matter, showing off for the edification of the less fortunate, can easily create bad lapses of taste and tact. As we saw with 'The Canonization' the ironic *anticipation* of those lapses by way of hyperbolic defiance, can often simply make matters worse. Yet, seen in the light of 'The Sunne Rising', that poem may have been attempting something more important than its actual achievement suggests, may have been meeting a very acute problem.

The trouble is that the feeling of passional fulfilment reaches us partly as a perception of its unthinkable rarity, so that the intrusive grain of self-satisfaction is already present. Tact, fineness of feeling, calls for some pretty delicate handling of the matter, therefore. For Donne, who is, as I've suggested, a congenital ironist, a fine salty self-mistrust keeps the obvious and embarrassing romantic excesses at bay; but in 'The Sunne Rising' he seems to me to have made something positive out of the temptations of the mode. He concedes that the lover's vaunt is intrinsically absurd, and concedes it through a cast of hyperbole so monumental that it simultaneously offers us the preposterous richness of the experience, and grants the impossibility of ever talking about it in ordinary language. And yet, at the same time, the lordly and delighted self-parody is presenting, in the most direct manner, an enormously heightened mental vivacity, a state of tremendous and exuberant stimulation. That stimulation, in a way, gives us most directly the 'content' of the love – not something soothing to the senses and lulling to the brain, not productive of ecstatic inarticulacy, but the kind of exaltation of feeling which heightens and sharpens every faculty and demands space to fling up its heels and knock its head against the stars. Donne isn't, as sometimes, trying to stimulate his feelings by means of the hyperbole; the attempt is rather to find some form of speech which is exaggerated *enough* to answer to the exaggeration, the opulence of his feelings. The sense of inexhaustible wealth, perfume, spicery, an insane profusion of natural bounty, all in one 'bed' ('*both* the'India's of spice and Myne' – one isn't enough) almost overwhelms him. And the presence of her generosity, the bounteousness of her body can only find expression in an image which makes her into a kind of universal courtesan (and thus laughingly recovers its self-possession by confessing the impossibility of ever describing her):

> Aske for those Kings whom thou saw'st yesterday,
> And thou shalt heare, All here in one bed lay.

Having come so far in the direction of overstatement and still falling far short of the mark, Donne reaches out, with a reckless abandon which is really the highest candour, and a tact towards both woman and reader, for the sole remaining hyperbole:

> She'is all States, and all Princes, I,
> Nothing else is.

Into the stunned silence which follows that – the short-line pause is masterly – the subsidiary outrages upon common sense fall with a faint bubble and ripple of laughter:

> Princes doe but play us; compar'd to this,
> All honor's mimique; All wealth alchimie.

And now the royal clemency can be extended to that faithful old retainer who had been bawled out at the opening of the poem. We return to the note, slightly parodied, of royal hauteur. But over the

73

last six lines a new kind of harmony is emerging. The world of the lovers is expanding to include the sun, and the world of the sun is contracting (but concentrating at the same time) until the two circumferences coincide – the sun's 'every where' finds its true human centre, and the lover's 'world' accepts the warmth of a real sun which, if it shines here to them, is also (therefore?) shining everywhere. And as that accommodation of heightened feeling to the commonplace daylight realities proceeds, the exalted manner subsides and a simpler geniality emerges, a geniality which finally stabilises the relation of the lovers to the world they necessarily defy. The stabilisation is projected as the sun is humorously readmitted to favour (permitted to bring breakfast in bed, as it were, to the young master and his new bride) and included in the lovers' felicity. The preposterousness of that, together with the calm assurance of tone, gives us the lovers' implacable defiance of daylight, sees it as impossible, and utterly refuses to abate one iota of the claim. The last line actually restates the brazen proclamation of 'Nothing else is', but with the vital difference that the proclamation is now held with a beautifully serious lightness. The bungled undertaking of 'The Canonization' – to show 'the whole worlds soule' epitomised in a love-relationship – is here carried to completion, as Donne finds that largely humorous, magnanimous tone in which the affirmation can justly be made:

> Thou sunne art halfe as happy'as wee,
> In that the world's contracted thus;
> Thine age askes ease, and since thy duties bee
> To warme the world, that's done in warming us.
> Shine here to us, and thou art every where;
> This bed thy center is, these walls, thy spheare.

It's an amazingly stable compound of crazy hyperbole and complete sobriety, beautifully equilibrated in the momentary stillness – the only still moment in the whole poem – of that last line.

Of course, that's not all there is to be said about fulfilled love and, in certain moods, one will probably feel there *is* something dubious about the public manner. 'Where does the real woman come into the picture?' one will grumble at such moments. 'Why is it that she is the States and Donne the Princes, and not the other way round?' But rather than continuing to grumble, it's better to turn over to 'The

74

Anniversarie' where, instead of concerning himself with loving splendidly, Donne ponders the difficulties of loving 'nobly'. The lovers are still resisting time, but not with that resonance of scorn ('houres, dayes, moneths, which are the rags of time'). Rather with a religious solemnity:

> This, no to morrow hath, nor yesterday,
> Running it never runs from us away,
> But truly keepes his first, last, everlasting day.

The lover doesn't speak out of the plenitude of the present merely to abuse the unruly old fool of a sun: time has soaked into the grain of his experience, and the sun which '*makes* times' (including the lovers' times) also, by the same act of transience, *un*makes them 'as they passe':

> The Sun it selfe, which makes times, as they passe,
> Is elder by a yeare, now, then it was
> When thou and I first one another saw.

And the pressure upon their sense of immunity from temporal process is very heavy indeed:

> All other things, to their destruction draw,
> Only our love hath no decay.

I think there's a note there which is quite foreign to 'The Sunne Rising'. Nothing in that poem has quite that tremulous delicacy or so fine a sense of the murderously poised alternatives between which love and trust must walk. And yet this poem, too, draws profoundly upon the common experience and the common metaphors. It has a rightness of utterance which is easier to recognise than describe, though perhaps one is most immediately conscious of it as a sustained steadiness of tone, long, eloquently modulated vocal lines, latent with powerful but subdued feeling.

The Anniversarie

> All Kings, and all their favorites,
> All glory of honors, beauties, wits,
> The Sun it selfe, which makes times, as they passe,
> Is elder by a yeare, now, then it was
> When thou and I first one another saw:
> All other things, to their destruction draw,

Only our love hath no decay;
This, no to morrow hath, nor yesterday,
Running it never runs from us away,
But truly keeps his first, last, everlasting day.

    Two graves must hide thine and my coarse,
      If one might, death were no divorce:
Alas, as well as other Princes, wee,
(Who Prince enough in one another bee,)
Must leave at last in death, these eyes, and eares,
Oft fed with true oathes, and with sweet salt teares;
    But soules where nothing dwells but love
(All other thoughts being inmates) then shall prove
This, or a love increased there above,
When bodies to their graves, soules from their graves
      remove.

    And then wee shall be throughly blest,
      But wee no more, then all the rest;
Here upon earth, we'are Kings, and none but wee
Can be such Kings, nor of such subjects bee;
Who is so safe as wee? where none can doe
Treason to us, except one of us two.
    True and false feares let us refraine,
Let us love nobly, and live, and adde againe
Yeares and yeares unto yeares, till we attaine
To write threescore: this is the second of our raigne.

The 'rightness' of that – as language, as gesture, as relationship – is
something I want, if I can, to push a little further towards definition.
The rightness is rightness about *something*: the poem directs us out-
wards to the quality of the love celebrated, not inwards to the mind of
the celebrating poet. But the rightness in the love has nothing to do
with codes of behaviour; it is not a matter of decorum in any external,
formal sense: readers who come to Donne with that expectation will
infallibly prove obtuse as Dryden was obtuse:

Donne affects the metaphysics...in his amorous verses where nature only
should reign; and perplexes the minds of the fair sex with nice speculations of
philosophy, when he should engage their hearts, and entertain them with the
softnesses of love.

That, as Grierson rightly objected,[1] is irredeemably vulgar – apart

[1] 'Introduction' to *Metaphysical Lyrics and Poems of the Seventeenth Century*, p. xx.

from being insulting to 'the fair sex' in a manner more far-reaching than Donne ever aspired to. There's something positively gentlemanly about his curt 'Hope not for mind in women...' beside this whited sepulchre of decaying courtesy. No; when Donne gets his tone wrong – as he often does – it is not because he is ignorant of the polite way to address a lady. He gets it wrong because, if you are addressing a real woman and have any sense of her existence which is at all lively, it's almost impossible to get it right. The state of exaltation and union for which the words come with a perfect inevitability and fitness, is probably as rare and transient in poetry as it is in nature; and the kind of mind which imagines it has this state as a perpetual possession or, worse, imagines it can simulate it by recourse to *manners*, is a mind far less scrupulous, far more anxious to feed itself with comfortable fictions, than Donne's.

But when he does get his tone right, one needs some more inward sense for the word 'decorum' to describe the achievement. A responsive fineness of a kind that cannot be codified or prescribed, but which exists 'in society' – what Lawrence called 'morality', 'that delicate, forever trembling and changing *balance* between me and my circumambient universe, which precedes and accompanies a true relatedness'.

In 'The Anniversarie' the poem's 'rightness' resides finally in its sensitive measuring of all *a priori* attitudes, all the possible stances that impinge on the poem from outside the relationship, against its own implicit human criteria; but the social and the personal are not seen as antitheses. There is no fretful rejection (romantic) of all claims but those of love; nor a craven submission (neo-classical, Drydenish) of the inner necessity of love to the canons of a tyrannical society. Instead there is a recognition (Donne's) that the integrity of love can only be seen as an integrity within the network of relations that surround it – kings and their favourites, honours, beauties, wits, the sun itself, death and infidelity. Love must find its wholeness by accepting all these conditioning factors; and that acceptance, I suggest, accounts more than anything else for the steadiness and assurance of tone which Donne is able to command. In an age still dominated too much by the romantic antithesis between the social and the personal, that tone ought to be a matter of some interest to us.

For 'The Anniversarie', the world outside intractably *is*. And it pursues its inexorable course, presided over by that paradigm of the temporal, the sun. But to love is to be involved in an activity which is, nevertheless, *sui generis*, not finally subject to reductive generality, for 'none but wee/Can be such Kings'. Starting from this point, the temptation to which all celebratory love poetry is prone, is to erect, upon the uniqueness, a doctrine of transcendence – which cuts the love off from those very warm and fleshly realities upon which it depends for its validation. On a hasty reading, 'The Anniversarie' might appear to be doing just this ('Only our love hath no decay'). But the emphasis on 'Only' makes its point, especially in conjunction with the parallel stress-inversion in the previous line: '*All* other things, to their destruction *draw*' – and that's a powerful verb, 'draw', with its transitive force veiled but not annulled: they draw all other things along with them, '*Only* our love...' – the temerity is explicit and eloquent. Besides, this is the first stanza not the last. Donne begins with the assurance we might have expected him to end upon; and the next stanza begins, 'Two graves...' Above all, there is that structural paradox the poem never deserts: the 'everlasting day' of love began exactly one year ago: 'This, no to morrow hath, nor yesterday'; yet Donne begins by looking back with profound gratitude on the yesterday 'When thou and I first one another saw', and ends by looking forward to the tomorrow when their reign will have stretched to the limits of life. The very notion of celebrating an 'Anniversarie' at all involves a cheerful acceptance of the before and after.

The position Donne adopts towards the temporal flux is a very special one. It's neither the limiting erotic naturalism of some of the *Elegies*, nor is it an amorous transcendentalism that spurns the physical realities, but something drawing upon both, finer than both, and ultimately utterly different from them both.

But this is not 'The Sunne Rising' either. The extremely moving *non sequitur* between the end of the first, and the beginning of the second, stanza makes that plain. Without warning, the measured royalty of utterance and image, the gravity, the solemnity, give way to a bleakly undramatic contemplation of death. Donne offers no explanation. But the absence of explanatory links says eloquently enough, 'Of course, this is the thought which always underlies our claims to permanence, the thought I see rising in your eyes, and which I can only meet with complete simplicity':

> Two graves must hide thine and my coarse,
> If one might, death were no divorce.

Behind the passing reference to some social complication which prevents their ever being husband and wife, one senses a frightening simplicity of contemplation and a complete composure of feeling. There's no writhing, none of the horrified fascination with decay and corruption we find elsewhere in Donne. Clean, inevitable, final, simple it is. No more. It is something to be accepted, and accepted partly because it unites the lovers with the rest of humanity, the common lot:

> Alas, as well as other Princes, wee,
> (Who Prince enough in one another bee,)
> Must leave at last in death, these eyes, and eares,
> Oft fed with true oathes, and with sweet salt teares.

The poise of that is very close to the poise of the late *Hymnes*, the same self-possessed calm which is not complacency, not a deprivation of feeling, not stony, but sentient and warmly alive to the fleshly reality of 'eyes and ears', the 'sweet salt teares' – the *tasted* tears of touch and embrace. One grasps the magnitude and the importance of the later, religious, renunciation ('I sacrifice this Iland unto thee,/And all whom I loved there, and who lov'd mee') all the better for hearing it foreshadowed here in a lover's meditation upon death: the dignity of the renunciation, in both cases, depends wholly upon the depth and purity of the love, the human love. What distinguishes 'The Anniversarie' from 'A Hymne to Christ', though, bringing it to its concluding resolution to 'love nobly, and live', and not to the Hymne's 'Everlasting night', is the achievement in the poem of a fully mutual 'we' – something never reached in Donne's relations with his divine lover. It's not, in 'The Anniversarie', the poet-prince ruling his mistress-state, but the trust of two very mortal creatures 'Who Prince enough in one another bee'. And the assured mutuality is borne to us through the quite palpable concern with what she must be feeling as he says these necessary, hard things.

I think the awareness that they *are* hard motivates the move to erect the 'everlasting day' upon a new religious foundation. The argument is from probabilities, not certainties – 'Surely it must be so' is the pressing, urgent note of the lines; and the thought draws

Donne further and further away from 'these eyes and eares', and towards the doctrine it has been the poem's distinction, so far, to avoid. Death, momentarily, ceases to be the great mysterious consummation and the saddening seal upon their separateness, and becomes instead a liberation from the clog of fleshly existence – 'When bodies to their graves, soules from their graves remove.' The body, that is to say, is the grave of the soul. This is somewhat pat, with its neat prepositional antithesis, 'bodies *to*…soules *from*'; and the confidence, anyway, such as it is, rests on a somewhat equivocal play with the word 'dwells' – 'soules where nothing *dwells* but love/(All other thoughts being inmates)' – which is to say, a good deal else besides love can be *found* in these souls, but since it is only temporarily resident there, as an 'inn-mate', it doesn't count. There is more than a trace of that filmy conditional feeling that haunted the ending of 'The Good-Morrow'. Something is being covered up. Yet in a way similar to that poem, it is so imperfectly covered up that the poetry can continue to work as a perfectly natural movement of the mind, recoiling away from painful possibilities it cannot wholly bring itself to face.

If there is some gravitation here towards those delusive 'essential' truths (truths which nevertheless leave out of account the pain of leaving 'in death, these eyes and eares'), it would seem to be placed when we arrive at the culminating 'affirmation', and the note turns out to be not one of triumph so much as of a puzzled musing– 'And then wee shall be throughly blest'. There is an infinitesimal pause, a hesitancy, and the puzzlement articulates itself delicately and tentatively: 'But wee no more, then all the rest'. Is this what you, what *we* really want? Haven't we lost something essential along the way? 'Throughly blest' we may be in heaven, but there is a kind of beatitude open to us only 'Here upon earth'. And it is to this blessedness that the warmth of the poem is now drawn.

The heavenly fulfilment is not annulled or retracted; it simply fades out of consideration as Donne brings into focus the princely existence human love has given them, a royal life that is possible because of the unique selfhood which makes every love a reality of its own, subject to its own laws, not ultimately referable to any other jurisdiction:

> Here upon earth, we'are Kings, and none but wee
> Can be such Kings, nor of such subjects bee.

With fine ironic steadiness, Donne gives us simultaneously the hyperbolic feelings ('none but wee/Can be such Kings') and the perfectly mundane, literal truth it contains (since they wish for no other empire than each other, their monarchy is of course unique). Both levels of feeling are true, and they reinforce each other: that very contentment with the personal fulfilment *makes* them 'Kings'. And the mutuality is nicely caught in the double syntax – none but we can be kings over such subjects, or subjects under such kings.

The one great mystery of creation is the irreplaceable, inexplicable individual being, and love is the relationship in which that mystery of selfhood finds both its resolution and its highest expression. That, too, is what makes them kings of nature. Better than kings:

> Who is so safe as wee? where none can doe
> Treason to us...

(then momentaneously the landscape is overcast by an ominous cloud)

> *except* one of us two.

And for an instant it looks as if the whole structure of the poem is tottering as Donne, by the logic of his own metaphor, is assailed by that nagging, gnawing inner suspicion that haunts so much of his love poetry – 'treason'. Treason in love.

The way he deals with this insinuating meanness of suspicion (a suspicion so personal as to cut him off, at a single stroke, from the reality of the woman, plunging him into horrible introversion) is one of his triumphs – a triumph not just of poetry, but of human dignity. He senses something ignoble about that fear. He is too just an observer of his own, and of human, nature to fall to resounding protestations that the fear is false; but neither will he be demeaned by harbouring the suspicion. There is only one thing to do with this kind of dishonourable fear – shake it off, or, in Donne's less melodramatic, more tactful word, 'refraine'.

> True *and* false feares let us refraine,

(whether true *or* false, they are ignoble)

> Let us love nobly,

(as befits princes in love, who can afford to be magnanimous)

> and live,

(not merely supinely expecting to be blest 'there above')

> and adde againe
> Yeares and yeares unto yeares, till we attaine
> To write threescore...

(gently deflating the 'everlastingness' of the opening by a reminder that there is less than a life-span left to them; but, to return to the entirely *un*conjectural, the warm reality to which the poem has now circled back, and in which all the misgivings and fears now founder, though they do not wholly disappear)

> ...this is the second of our raigne.

That's a fairly substantial modification of the opening claims. But Donne has established on the way something that is more important than any kind of everlastingness – the royalty, the princeliness, the nobility of the relationship. It is a 'raigne', and this is its second year – a fact that neither death, the necessary divorce of their affections, conjectures about the after-life, nor the 'true and false feares' of infidelity can finally destroy. With a fulness nobody could have foreseen, the paradoxical doctrine 'that the gifts of the Body are better than those of the Minde' has come to fruition. Donne will have no hankering after an everlastingness which, in a sense, they already possess – 'Running' our love may be, but 'it never runs from *us* away'. Felicity of the *soul* alone would lack the specific edge which makes joys whole, 'Here upon earth' where 'none but wee/Can be such Kings'. And if the condition of reality in love turns out to be a submission to the passage of the years, then let us solemnly, soberly, joyfully celebrate their passing – 'This is the second of our raigne'. Human limitation is so richly embraced that it dissolves itself, as limitation, and is reconstituted as the whole, the only, the 'right' feeling, both natural and just.

I suppose it will be clear by now that the Donne I'm advancing for our most serious attention is not a spectacular pyrotechnician who is continually startling us out of *our* wits, as a way of reconciling us to *his*. His surprises are of a more deeply satisfying kind – 'that comprehension and expense of thought which at once fills the whole mind, and of which the first effect is sudden astonishment, and the second rational admiration' – Johnson's version of the sublime.

And yet one might be 'surprised' in the superficial sense to learn that the author of 'The Sunne Rising' also wrote 'A Valediction: forbidding Mourning'; surprised, that is, before the astonishment gave way to rational admiration, and before one came to realise that the poem is another variant on the common theme of 'loving nobly'. In overt sense, the two poems are very different. 'The Sunne Rising' celebrates reckless self-giving, sensual liberation and physical liberality, the breaking down of restraint. The 'Valediction' celebrates, with the same poise, natural reticence, restraint, the courteous withholding of emotion. I say *natural* reticence quite deliberately – although at this moment in erotic history the phrase may sound rather odd. But the argument of the poem is that there is a logic in the very nature of passion which exacts this restraint – not a restraint *upon* emotion, but a natural restraint arising from the emotion itself – a natural fear of what Donne calls, with great exactitude, 'prophanation':

> T'were prophanation of our joyes
> To tell the layetie our love.

That gets beautifully the sense one has, about almost all public displays of emotion, that something is being cheapened. Feelings are being relieved, but losing their purity and integrity in the process. (It's a protest against that cheapening, a protest itself borne down in the swelling tide of emotion, that we are given, I think, in 'A Valediction: Of Weeping'.) That kind of violence of emotion, the earthquake of feeling, is no true index of the *depth* of feeling – its tumultuousness is misleading. The really cataclysmic feelings may be imperceptible to the naked eye:

> Moving of th'earth brings harmes and feares,
> Men reckon what it did and meant,
> But trepidation of the spheares,
> Though greater farre, is innocent.

'Innocence', in this context, is anything but some innocuous absence of hurtful properties: the magnitude of the 'trepidation' is what makes for the 'innocence'. It is the same with the terrible fact of the lovers' impending separation: it may be a kind of death, but it ought not to recall the vain and unseemly threshings of a dying sinner; rather the calm passing of a good man, something in which his own soul acquiesces. It is a holy mystery, and a great grief, but one about which the 'sad friends' can only speculate.

> As virtuous men passe mildly away,
> And whisper to their soules, to goe,
> Whilst some of their sad friends doe say,
> The breath goes now, and some say, no:
>
> So let us melt, and make no noise...

'Melt', again, is the beautifully exact, the irresistibly right, word – the last evanescent pressure of the hand, and then dissolution apart. And at the same time a very strong suggestion of the warming and softening that the parting involves, as if they were melting *together*, fusing.

The quick of tender feeling is in that second stanza, and the rest grows from it. Half jocularly, Donne moves on to 'arguefy', gently parodying the sense of superiority with which they are supporting their resolution not to make a scene: 'Dull sublunary lovers' love, compared to our pure super-celestial love...(one can't *say* this, of course, and both of us understand that we can't, but your part in me and in my feelings makes it possible for me to say it at least to you– for between us it has a certain kind of truth)...'Dull sublunary lovers' love

> (Whose soule is sense) cannot admit
> Absence, because it doth remove
> Those things which elemented it.

But *we*...' It's not so much that he wants to impose the neo-platonic fiction of the union of two souls upon her – the tone is much too wry for that ('a love, so much refin'd,/That our *selves* know what it is) – as that it is a necessary fiction if they are not to profane their joys. 'Surely,' Donne says, and with a kind of urgency presses it upon her, 'surely we...'

> Inter-assured of the mind,
> Care lesse, eyes, lips, and hands to misse.

But there's a plangency there which belies the assurance ('Care *lesse*', not 'Care not'). His mind lingers over those 'eyes, lips, and hands', so that the 'to misse' comes out with a faint note of interrogation and pain. And in the next stanza, this argument for *firmness* declares itself as a beautiful but flimsy thing:

> Our two soules therefore, which are one,
>   Though I must goe, endure not yet
> A breach, but an expansion,

– and notice now aptly the mere logic is, pointing, in the word 'expansion', to painful enlargement, distension (tantamount, in point of feeling, to the anguish of constriction), thus setting up a tension against the hypothesis –

> Like gold to ayery thinnesse beate.

'Beate' hints at the acute yet delicate agony which produces the beauty of love-in-absence. But it is an attenuation, something which a breath of wind can destroy. It's not what ought to follow from real 'inter-assurance'.

Donne accepts the logic of his image: the two souls, then, cannot be one; there is something more solid about their relationship than that tissue of gold. There is some real connexion which no absence can destroy nor attenuate. Change in one is registered in the other. They are like 'stiffe twin compasses' – 'stiffe' in enduring their suffering silently; 'stiffe' like the wooden compasses, in that it takes an ugly and clumsy violation to force them apart; 'stiffe' also because Donne is conceding that an absurd stiffness is being forced upon them in parting and he lets that be a shared awareness between them.

Upon that shared wryness he can build the entirely serious activity by which he defines their mutuality:

> Thy soule the fixt foot, makes no show
>   To move, but doth, if the'other doe.

(The air of lecture-room demonstration is not a Donne mannerism, but a part of the poem's courteous restraint.) We now discover what this 'firmnes' is, that he has been urging upon her: not insentience, irresponsiveness, but the responsive stability of the 'fixt foot' of the compass. Like the unseen trepidation of the spheres, its real movement may be 'greater farre' than the more obvious movements of grief-at-separation; but it rests in its own proper centrality, making 'no *show* / To move...'

I have never understood why this image should have been the subject of so much puzzled and querulous comment. Surely the first thing one registers is its perfect aptness – at least in point of logic. It meets all the objections the anaalogy of beaten gold was open to: what, in all this uniform 'expansion' of material, has become of the 'two soules'? what possible relation can this spatial metaphor have to the woman who sits at home and the man who travels? in what sense is it anything more than a specious gloss upon the pain of being separated? how long can the gold hope to endure no breach, if the expansion goes on? Apart from uniting movement and immobility, separation and unity, the compasses are solid sensible objects which really belong to the world where a lover's business may call him away from his most important allegiances.

But hard on the heels of that perception of the *logical* fitness comes the realisation of the fitness in point of feeling:

> And though it in the center sit,

– and notice the simple visualised exactness of 'sit': the woman left at home to her thoughts and her solitude, Penelope without a loom –

> Yet when the other far doth rome,

– performing his prosaic, mechanical, yet necessary function –

> It leanes, and hearkens after it,
> And growes erect, as that comes home.

– 'home', again, giving us both the geometry and the domestic reality it figures. But 'leanes, and hearkens after it' . . . One could hardly have suspected that so much yearning tenderness could have been concentrated in so mechanical an image, but there it is. And a tenderness clean and unsentimental by reason of the functionalism of the metaphor. Unobtrusively but powerfully, each word carries its full charge of meaning: as with the word 'hearkens' which eloquently fuses the physical 'hearkening *after*' the departed lover (the woman always leaning in the direction he has gone) and the state of mind which is always 'hearkening after' news.

The subtlety of thought and feeling is borne in a speech movement which is serene, limpid, domestic, both equable and powerful in its understatement of emotion. In fact, one way of describing the poem's very special quality would be to point to the rich context it provides for a term *like* 'domestic'. (Don't fear, that isn't the ghost of Ann More returning to haunt us; I just want to pay my respects to the created reality, in the poem, of those two calm lovers who are 'Inter-assured of the mind'.)

The last stanza returns to the poem's point of departure, the moment of the lover's departure. That reunited embrace, when the travelling partner comes 'home', is still far in the future; the compass is tracing the 'just' circle which is only possible by virtue of her 'firmnes'. His going away is 'oblique', off, fetching a vast circle to return to the point he should never have left; but he must go (the rhyming stress on 'must' insists that they both know this), and, after all,

> Thy firmnes *makes* my circle just.

That line catches up almost everything the poem has been saying: 'without that firmness I've been urging on you (and which we have now achieved) my going away would be deeply *un*just, since I cannot leave you in hopeless distress; but when I know you are being firm, here at home, there is some hope of my being just while I am away from you, just to your love and to its claims upon me even in absence; and even that circuit which I make *away* from you is just as long as it is centred upon you.' The richness of meaning that clusters around those words 'firmnes' and 'just' is inexhaustible, more easily felt than explained by Empsonian ambiguities. 'Justice' by way of 'firmnes' is the poem's whole goal and ideal.

And then, in the last line, Donne conflates the two usages of the compass analogy in such a way as to desert the strict analogy in the interests of a gesture of deep and affectionate farewell:

> Thy firmnes makes my circle just,
> And makes me end, where I begunne.

As the line refers to the concluding of the poem, we might read, 'There is nothing to be said. I end where I began – conscious above all of the need to avoid all 'noise'. The poem, consummated in your 'firmnes', must consign itself to silence. But to 'end where I begunne' is also to return physically to her after his journey, she being now (impossibly in terms of strict analogy, but pressingly as the woman he loves) both the centre of the circle and the point on the circumference from which he sets out: 'All my movements, centred upon the fact of what you are, and that you are *here*, can be no more than a describing of circles which will come to a close on you as their centre *and* their point of departure. You are, in your firmness, the beginning and ending of all I do.'

One paraphrases with a kind of desperation, when there is so much that might be missed, and when paraphrasing is so excellent a way of missing it. What it may suggest, all the same, is the kind of fulness the plainest words can take on in the mind, if we will allow them the imaginative space they demand, and if we will read the poem with that pondering, yet not ponderous, gravity which makes its halting, elusively-stressed movement so eloquent:

A Valediction: forbidding Mourning
As virtuous men passe mildly away,
    And whisper to their soules, to goe,
Whilst some of their sad friends doe say,
    The breath goes now, and some say, no:

So let us melt, and make no noise,
    No teare-floods, nor sigh-tempests move,
T'were prophanation of our joyes
    To tell the layetie our love.

Moving of th'earth brings harmes and feares,
    Men reckon what it did and meant,
But trepidation of the spheares,
    Though greater farre, is innocent.

Dull sublunary lovers' love
    (Whose soule is sense) cannot admit
Absence, because it doth remove
    Those things which elemented it.

But we by a love, so much refin'd,
    That our selves know not what it is,
Inter-assured of the mind,
    Care lesse, eyes, lips, and hands to misse.

Our two soules therefore, which are one,
    Though I must goe, endure not yet
A breach, but an expansion,
    Like gold to ayery thinnesse beate.

If they be two, they are two so
  As stiffe twin compasses are two,
Thy soule the fixt foot, makes no show
  To move, but doth, if the'other doe.

And though it in the center sit,
  Yet when the other far doth rome,
It leanes, and hearkens after it,
  And growes erect, as that comes home.

Such wilt thou be to mee, who must
  Like th'other foot, obliquely runne;
Thy firmnes makes my circle just,
  And makes me end, where I begunne.

If space were unlimited, this would be the moment to turn over to the 'Song: Sweetest love, I do not goe' where, with a greater dramatic directness, Donne faces the woman's grief at parting and searches his soul for the wholly tactful, tender, yet manly way of meeting it. We are watching the 'interassurance of the mind' being fought for and won, reclaimed from the encroachments of a grief too personal and dependent to be just, but too deep to be ignored. The marriage of strength and gentleness gives rise to a poem which is both a dramatic encounter and a pure flight of song. But space is not unlimited, and another of the *Songs and Sonets*, very different in temper from either the 'Valediction' or the 'Song', claims our attention. I'm thinking of 'Aire and Angels'.

'Aire and Angels' is a poem that seems often to defeat, baffle, or rile its readers; not so much because of its difficult argument or abstruse allusions (a note on the physiology of the Elizabethan angel clears them up fairly smartly), but, I suspect, because readers frequently don't recognise the realm of experience out of which the poem is written.

Donne, in this poem, is plainly placing a very high value upon preserving some essential detachment at the heart of an emotional involvement. Even at the moment of frank self-giving, he wishes to know exactly what it is that he does. It's open to us, of course, to read this as dishonestly self-withholding, and to see the detachment as a betrayal of love. But if we do we will have missed something rare and irreplaceable.

I think I can help to create a suitable climate for the poem by making a detour into Henry James' fiction: from *The Wings of the Dove*, an encounter between those two exceedingly civilised lovers, Kate Croy and Merton Densher. Densher has been telling Kate of his less than *comme-il-faut* childhood and youth as the son of a peregrinatory army chaplain, fearing that he is altogether too shop-soiled to meet her naturally high requirements. Kate refuses to be dismayed by this deplorably chequered past and 'when she had had it from beginning to end she declared that she now made out more than ever yet of what she loved him for'. Merton, however, insists on apologising for his dubious antecedents:

brave enough though his descent to English earth, he had passed, by the way, through zones of air that had left their ruffle on his wings, had been exposed to initiations ineffaceable. Something had happened to him that could never be undone.

When Kate Croy said to him as much he besought her not to insist, declaring that this indeed was what was too much the matter with him, that he had been but too probably spoiled for native, for insular use. On which, not unnaturally, she insisted the more, assuring him, without mitigation, that if he was complicated and brilliant she wouldn't for the world have had him anything less; so that he was reduced in the end to accusing her of putting the dreadful truth to him in the hollow guise of flattery. She was making out how abnormal he was in order that she might eventually find him impossible: and, as she could fully make it out but with his aid, she had to bribe him by feigned delight to help her. If her last word for him, in the connection, was that the way he saw himself was just a precious proof the more of his having tasted of the tree and being thereby prepared to assist her to eat, this gives the happy tone of their whole talk...[1]

In a context where love is made on the understanding that 'if he was complicated and brilliant she wouldn't for the world have had him anything less', we can expect the exchanges to have an edge, even a danger, which in another context might seem flippant, or unfeeling – if it weren't for the palpable 'happy tone of their whole talk', which reveals upon what a profound mutual appreciation the exchanges of wit are founded (and that bears very directly on the tone and atmosphere of 'Aire and Angels'). And if we were to assume that the ironic

[1] Book Second, ch. 4.

edge on their exchanges made the expression of deep emotion impossible, we would be deeply mistaken.

He went on with that fantasy, but at this point Kate ceased to attend. He saw after a little that she had been following some thought of her own, and he had been feeling the growth of something determinant even through the extravagance of much of the pleasantry, the warm, transparent irony, into which their livelier intimacy kept plunging like a confident swimmer. Suddenly she said to him with extraordinary beauty: 'I engage myself to you for ever.'

The beauty was in everything, and he could have separated nothing – couldn't have thought of her face as distinct from the whole joy. Yet her face had a new light. 'And I pledge you – I call God to witness! – every spark of my faith; I give you every drop of my life.' That was all, for the moment, but it was enough, and it was almost as quiet as if it were nothing. They were in the open air, in an alley of the Gardens; the great space, which seemed to arch just then higher and spread wider for them, threw them back into deep concentration....

To read 'Aire and Angels' we have to develop ears which can hear what is being said through the 'extravagance of much of the pleasantry', and eyes that can see through 'the warm, transparent irony' to the 'extraordinary beauty' which is so wholly self-possessed that it is 'almost as quiet as if it were nothing'. In fact it is the quietness of deep concentration, at the end of the poem, which is often mistaken for a lame and bungled conclusion.

We begin very much as we did in 'The Good-Morrow' with some review of of what 'thou and I/Did, till we lov'd'; but this is a very different poem – the hearts, though true, are not at all plain. One is tempted to add that neither do they know each other as well as the lovers of 'The Good-Morrow', except that the 'livelier intimacy' of 'Aire and Angels' makes the comparison a tricky one, and it's probably best to reserve judgment. In fact, more than most, this poem requires to be read backwards if we are register the precise note of the first stanza. Only then does the figurative play with the notion of an angelic haunting lose that suspicion of frivolity and show its true function.

To praise in the kind of superlatives Donne envisages here is to run the risk of being merely and embarrassingly effusive. Tact means both preserving his own dignity, and offering the praise with a lightness which is gallant enough to permit the woman a smiling acceptance, yet serious and ardent enough not to strike a false note of ugly and self-conscious flippancy. Yet he can't launch blindly into ecstatic celebration ('Ev'ry thy haire for love to worke upon/Is much too much...'), for that would be to lay her gratitude under contribution in rather gross ways. Instead Donne offers something that is clearly a compliment – the suggestion that the encounter with her is an act of recognition, giving final shape to an intuition hitherto haunting, but 'shapelesse' – but offers it with a figurative lightness which is as courteously open to a graceful refusal as to a gracious acceptance.

The earlier loves become hovering, half-perceived, numinous presences, 'a voice', 'a shapelesse flame'; but the implication that neither the mind nor the man can rest content with these imperfect epiphanies is amused enough at itself to leave the woman unencumbered by his desire of her, at the same time as she cannot fail to be aware of its existence.

> Twice or thrice had I loved thee,
> Before I knew thy face or name;
> So in a voice, so in a shapelesse flame,
> *Angells* affect us oft, and worship'd bee;
>   Still when, to where thou wert, I came,
> Some lovely glorious nothing I did see.

'Worship'd' both is, and is not, a part of the play of wit here: there *is* a genuinely reverential tremor in the verse movement, but the tone is flexible enough to take in as well the incipient comic dismay of the 'lovely glorious nothing' with which female beauty has fobbed him off in the past. The anti-climax leads at once to the deft mobilisation of an argument, from the fundamental constitution of man's nature, to a necessity of incarnating the 'angelic' vision:

> But since my soule, whose child love is,
> Takes limmes of flesh, and else could nothing doe,
>   More subtile then the parent is,
> Love must not be, but take a body too.

The fantasticated logic, with its illicit playing upon literal meanings for the figurative 'child' and 'parent', is a kind of verbal love-play, lightly affectionate in its actual gestures; but the beloved is free to read in it all the deeper feelings of which it might be a token. And the logical orderliness is the mark of a self-restraint in which she can put perfect confidence. The tone becomes even more weightily judicious:

> And therefore what thou wert, and who,
>   I bid Love aske, and now
> That it assume thy body, I allow,
> And fixe it selfe in thy lip, eye, and brow.

'Brow' is exactly right for the reverential, yet affectionate distance which is still preserved between them. The stanza ends with a beautifully measured *ritenuto* and a pause of expressive stillness.

Only now does Donne feel free to reveal the depth of his own feeling. In a pattern that's becoming familiar by now, the new stanza simply sheds the *gallant* and slightly mannered air of the last and gives itself freely up to the passion Donne has shown himself capable of controlling and is therefore free now to express. It is real and overwhelming passion, something that has him foundering beneath a cargo of pleasures too rich and abundant for one small vessel to carry. The bewilderment is real. But so is that grain of urbane self-possession which mocks at himself for imagining that such 'wares' could ever serve for 'ballast', and offers the comic spectacle of his foundering pinnace as the truest tribute he can pay to the woman's beauty. The bewilderment is consciously enjoyed, and the self-possession is gladly surrendered in a single complex act of self-giving. An act of extraordinary beauty.

> Whilst thus to ballast love, I thought,
> And so more steddily to have gone,
> With wares which would sinke admiration,
> I saw, I had loves pinnace overfraught,
>   Ev'ry thy haire for love to worke upon
> Is much too much, some fitter must be sought.

The gift too great for the receiver is accepted without false modesty and without bravado as the 'extreme and scatt'ring bright' thing it is – scattering, diffusing, shattering consciousness with its brilliance, but at the same time brilliantly refracting the visionary light in a way which multiplies and intensifies it. It is the full revelation of that initial 'glorious nothing'.

His difficulty before was that his love had no body; his difficulty now is that it has such a body that he can see nothing else. On neither condition can love 'inhere' – and that, the full incarnation of the ideal and the visionary, is the goal the poem has set itself. 'Some fitter must be sought', a fitter body for love, or else a fitter lover for her.

Donne turns again to the Angel analogy, but with a new intent: 'Then as an Angell, face, and wings/Of aire, not pure as it, yet pure doth weare' – it sounds like a new incarnation for the angel-vision of the opening, but there is one entirely new element – 'So *thy love* may be my loves spheare.' Given 'thy love', the opposition of the purely spiritual (which was insubstantial) and the incarnated (which overwhelmed with plenitude) is resolved, for the dualism of soul and body is itself dissolved: each 'love' is the act of the total being, soul *and* body – and the loves are related as two enabling manifestations of the same reality, he moving within her love, she within his, in two mutually enclosing spheres. Or at least, it *may* be that, for the precise allocation of 'angell' and 'aire' to her and his loves is deliberately and impenetrably obscure. It doesn't come clear, until the very last line, that the analogy is to be at the expense of 'womens love'.

A remark of Conrad's bears very much on that ending. 'A woman's true tenderness,' he says, 'like the true virility of a man, is expressed in action of a conquering kind.' I suggest that what we have in that final gesture is a true tenderness (also a true virility) expressing itself in action of a conquering kind. Love must be made to 'inhere', not merely in the hypothetical way that the metaphorical resolution propounds, but actively and in terms of the dramatised relationship the poem has set up. It cannot desert the warm, transparent ironies in which it is rooted. Nor can it do itself justice as a state of visionary blindness, 'scatt'ring bright'. And if the love is to inhere it must do so on the terms that a merely human, and fully human, man/woman relationship permits.

And so we get a return to the lighter tone of the opening, though it is now a charged lightness, to the language of the war of the sexes and the competition of love. It is a calculated and beautifully graded descent. The note of dominance (not hammered, but deftly touched into sound) is a part of the total compliment, a tribute to her wit and detachment, her freedom from vanity – and a tribute, in that it offers to her, as part of his deeply civilised gallantry, the necessary ingredient of his own male egoism, the impulse to conquest which answers to her different woman's egoism, resonates with it, as it were. They are, like Kate and Merton, two equals enjoying supremely the fact that they are not each other, not one soul, but beautifully distinct, beautifully civilised, and beautifully free to make the gift of themselves to each other. It is a smile of complete understanding and complete self-possession that passes between them.

5

'Analytick Attempts'
Songs and Sonets III

A man is rarely content to rest in the wholly implicit – not even when it's as richly present as it is in the great lyrics of the *Songs and Sonets*. He is driven by a necessary, yet specious passion for intellectual structure, a rage of annexation lest the richly implicit escape him along with the moment that contains it. He wants what is now, and wholly, true, to be hereafter and forever Truth. And in the pursuit of substantive doctrine he is liable to lose the meaning.

Donne's passion for intellectual structure, his quest for a philosophy of love, has some of this disquieting doubleness about it. The task had to be taken on, for what we cannot understand we may eventually lose the capacity even to experience; yet the results of merely 'understanding' love, when the wholeness of the human event is not fully honoured, can be disastrous. I suppose no one would deny that in the love-experience there are elements that can be roughly designated 'soul' and 'body', facets of a single complex reality which belongs properly to neither. But in a *doctrine* of love, soul and body almost inevitably become alternatives to be chosen between, and one or other of them is bound to be degraded in the process:

> On man heavens influence workes not so,
> But that it first imprints the ayre,
> Soe soule into the soule may flow,
> Though it to body first repaire.

So we're informed in 'The Extasie' – 'informed' being the operative word. The tone is level, expository, unemotive, the dry, colourless voice intimating plainly that the problem is propounded, and will be resolved, purely on the theoretic level. The resolution is correspondingly unsatisfactory. Consciously, Donne may be *resisting* the dichoto-

mising of soul and body when he sets out to define the role of the body
in love. But his very way of putting the question – What is the body's
function in the love-reality? – implies that it is some kind of interloper
whose presence has to be rationalised. The lines, in fact, are loaded
(however inadvertently) with insulting condescension to 'body'
which is, it appears, a mere transient instrument for the soul-reality
in which it cannot participate.

An alluring critical simplification would interpret the difficulty as
created by the very terms 'soul' and 'body', and would proscribe them
accordingly as poetic outlaws. But the terms can have a living context.
They had it, for example, in 'Aire and Angels':

> But since my soule, whose child love is,
> Takes limmes of flesh, and else could nothing doe,
> More subtile then the parent is,
> Love must not be, but take a body too,
> And therefore what thou wert, and who,
> I bid Love aske…

That is also, I suppose, an account of the soul 'repairing' to the body.
But as a man who awaits the momentous incarnation of the 'lovely
glorious nothing' which has ravished and tantalised him, Donne does
not enjoy, here, the precise sense of orderly sequences, scientifically
discrete substances, and cool instrumentality which would permit him
a line (or a sentiment) like 'Though it to body first repaire'. He uses
the terms 'soul' and 'body' as a man who acknowledges his partici-
pation in both; not, as with 'The Extasie' quatrain, as a partisan of
the soul. And the words take consequent depth of colour from their
surroundings: they become something more than abstractions.

To put it another way, the 'doctrine' in the two passages – if one
can even use the word – is radically different. In 'Aire and Angels',
love was the child of the soul – an intimate, natural blood relation –
and it fulfilled its soul-nature by taking a body. It did not 'repaire' to
the body; it inhered. And we did not need, therefore, to be reassured
– it would have struck a grotesquely false note if we had been – that,
despite the regrettable interposition of the body, no actual contamina-
tion had taken place. The identification of flesh with contamination
was ruled out of order by the whole context of feeling. The two pas-
sages, despite the superficial resemblances, are almost antithetical in
feeling and sense.

I'm insisting on this distinction because real chaos can be made of Donne's poetry by assuming he was always of the same mind concerning the relations of soul and body; or that he always meant the same thing by the terms. One can then easily be led into follies like trying to gloss the rest of the *Songs and Sonets* in the light of 'The Extasie'. Given its labyrinthine argument and its treacherous shifts of tone (neither of which I've begun to discuss yet), that in itself would be no mean feat; but even if we took the dualism of this one stanza as the core of the 'doctrine', ignoring its context, and saw Donne as endorsing the higher, soul-love, we would still be met by flat contradictions elsewhere; as for instance in 'Loves Alchymie', which pours scorn on exactly 'The Extasie's kind of spiritualisation of love:

> That loving wretch that sweares,
> 'Tis not the bodies marry, but the mindes,
> Which he in her Angelique findes,
> Would sweare as justly, that he heares,
> In that dayes rude hoarse minstralsey, the spheares.

The 'loving wretch' is patently Donne himself, in poem after poem. This isn't a solitary example either: the whole argument of 'Loves Growth' rests on the proposition that

> Love's not so pure, and abstract, as they use
> To say, which have no Mistresse but their Muse,
> But as all else...elemented too...

So where does that leave us?

It's not a matter of discovering what Donne 'really believed'. Pretty clearly he found each account of love (the 'pure, and abstract' Platonic love and the 'elemented', inhering love) appealing in different ways and at different times. The unofficial dialogue between the two was never, to my knowledge, terminated. But it was brought to a pitch of unusual explicitness in 'The Extasie', a poem in which, to judge from the orderly marshalling of material and the overt formality of the debate, Donne set out to settle the matter once and for all.

Logical structure is, of course, no novelty in Donne's poetry; but the exhaustiveness of the argumentation in 'The Extasie' is unusual. The mind is not darting about in agile hyperactivity, but steadily accumulating analogies and data bearing on a single point; and when that first brief is complete, the same patient accumulation begins upon a second. It's probably this palpable intention to make a final statement, a summation, that is responsible more than anything else for the belief that 'The Extasie' is one of Donne's great poems. The exhaustiveness, combined with the logical perspicuity, ought to be impressive.

If we start with this overt structure, it all seems plain sailing: (1) Thesis: the ecstatic union of souls, its commodities and discommodities; (2) Antithesis: the claims of the body for satisfaction, giving rise to (3) Synthesis: the true relation between soul and body defined, followed by (4) a slow dissolve as 'we'are to bodies gone'. But immediately scruples arise. Isn't this altogether too suspiciously lucid? It's a commonplace of human psychology that wonders of clarification can be wrought by schematising, into sequence and series, mental happenings which are in fact simultaneous and indistinguishable. If the body did, in fact, lie mute while the soul reasoned itself into a *cul-de-sac*; and if the soul next, recognising its predicament, implored the body to develop *its* position; and if the mind then stepped tactfully between the disputants and proposed a mutually acceptable formula; then Donne's synthesis might be a matter of great human import. But as it is, one cannot be at all sure how authentic it is.

Donne is ready, of course, with the ironist's perennial defence: he *knows* the structure is flimsy. Not for one moment has he mistaken his hypothetical reconstruction for fact. The poem rejoices in a high degree of whimsical detachment from its own postulates. But the whimsy, by the same token, weakens the persuasive force of the arguments Donne appears to find so droll. If he cannot commit himself to his conclusions, is there any reason why we should?

And then there is the strange *non sequitur* of the ending, which seems to squirm out from under its own conclusions. We had been moving towards the synthetic identification of soul and body; then, suddenly, they're alternatives again, and we're exhorted to opt for the body – albeit in the name of the soul. Some readers have seen this as proof that the poem's basic objective is not synthesis but seduction (a view which implies some rather queer notions of female psychology: reading 'The Extasie' aloud would not seem likely, on the face of it, to have any markedly aphrodisiac effects).

If Donne is trying to seduce anyone, though, it is himself; and he seems not to be having much success. The exhortation, 'To'our bodies turne wee then' is immediately succeeded by a series of scratchily defensive justifications: 'that so/Weake men on love reveal'd may look' – one notes the tell-tale pun on 'revelation' as epiphany *and* nudity, and the unpleasantly toothy smile that goes with it. 'Loves mysteries in soules doe grow/*But yet* the body ...' The prickliness, the defensiveness seems almost to be parodying itself: 'Of course we do not do this for ourselves; it is purely for the edification of the less fortunate to whom this beatitude would otherwise be closed.' 'We ought not to undervalue the, as it were, physical; it has its humble place.' 'Do not imagine for one moment, my friend, that we are embarrassed by your presence, as we "to bodies go"; you will see "small change".' It is like 'The Canonization': the more deeply you look into the poem the more invisible the poet becomes. If this is not self-parody, that is only because it is something even more questionable.

But then a great deal else in 'The Extasie' is tinged with the same elusive mockery. The spiritual union of the opening section takes place in a setting of such absurd sensual over-ripeness that it inevitably comments dryly on the incongruous, violet-like modesty of the lovers:

> Where, like a pillow on a bed,
> A Pregnant banke swel'd up to rest ...

to rest what but 'The *violets* reclining head'? If the intention of this anti-climax, and of the hands 'firmely cimented/With a fast balme, which thence did spring', and of the grotesque conceit of the threaded eyeballs, and of the picture of the lovers as a pair of plaster 'sepulchrall statues' – if the intention of all this bizarre detail were merely to place their affectation of being above sex in an amusing and touching light, we might be able to take our bearings. At times something of a playful maturity which can afford to be indulgent does get into the lines:

> So to'entergraft our hands, as yet
> Was all the meanes to make us one,
> And pictures in our eyes to get
> Was all our propagation.

But that steady, warm amusement is constantly crossed by something colder and more cutting. The play of figure is so bizarre, so deeply compounded of coolness and animus, that no clear intent can be discerned – unless the title, designating the whole experience by one of the Elizabethan words for madness, was meant to provide the clue.

At this point the hypothetical specialist in love enters, one who 'by good love' is 'growen all minde' (a hydrocephalic vision of monstrous intellectual over-development flits across one's mind). Unlike Donne, this expert has no trouble with the diagnosis. He is familiar with the condition. And provided he stands (delicious touch!) 'Within convenient distance', he can *hear* the inaudible speech of the two-souls-which-are-one. And he goes away, or might go away, Donne assures us, almost ecstatic himself, purified by the high truths he has been privileged to overhear.

> If any, so by love refin'd,
>   That he soules language understood,
> And by good love were growen all minde,
>   Within convenient distance stood,
> He (though he knew not which soule spake,
>   Because both meant, both spake the same)
> Might thence a new concoction take,
>   And part farre purer then he came.

That might well be Donne's impish gibe at the Florentine Professors of Love, the amorous theoreticians who had set up academies for instruction in such matters. But again the bearing of the wit is obscure, and the amplification of the neo-platonic doctrine runs on through so many lines, and through so many baffling shifts of tone – from the mock clarification of 'Wee see by this, it was not sexe,/Wee see, we saw not what did move', with its unmistakable tokens that somebody is being guyed ('Wee see, we saw, Margery Daw'), to the comparatively assured weightiness of 'When love, with one another so/Interanimates two soules ...', weight being a function there of something more than the polysyllable – that there is finally no way to distinguish an authorial position, or even be sure of an authorial presence. The irony has become defensive, a retreat upon private intent, titterings behind closed doors at subjects undisclosed.

We snatch with relief, consequently, at the first solid sentiment that presents itself ('solid', that is, provided we turn a blind eye to its ironic placing right on the heels of the souls' alleged perfection, which 'no change can invade'):

> But O alas, so long, so farre
> Our bodies why doe wee forbeare?

But immediately that niggling, qualifying, problematical voice re-
turns: 'They are *ours*, though they are not *wee* ... Nor are *drosse* to us,
but *allay* ... *Though* it to body first repaire ... *But yet* the body is his
booke ...'

If I could believe that the pompous magnanimity so beautifully
caught in these grudging concessions – if I could believe this had
slipped from Donne unawares, absorbed as he was in higher things,
there would be no problem. We would then read the poem, Mil-
tonically as it were, for its conscious intent only, and the dramatic
commentary on that intention – a commentary supplied largely
through the tone – would have to be discounted. But this is a very
odd way to read Donne. Since it is at least equally possible that he, too,
is amused by the soul's ponderous gravity in conceding to the body
what it is in no position ever to withold, and amused by the body's
needlessly craven submission to a tyrannical and intransigent soul, I
can't quite shake off the suspicion that he is also amused by the redun-
dancy of the whole debate. The poem, on this reading, becomes a
gigantic burlesque (though at times a genial one) of the neo-platonic
dichotomising which fetches this vast dialectical circle to arrive back
home at the ineffably obvious: 'To'our bodies turne wee then.' If we
balk at this reading, I suspect it's less because it is inherently impro-
bable, than because we lack the ironic stamina to see it through all
seventy-six lines. Donne – there is nothing surer – possessed that
stamina.

The only real obstacle to the reading that I can see lies in the two
quatrains for which the poem is most justly famous:

> As our blood labours to beget
>   Spirits, as like soules as it can,
> Because such fingers need to knit
>   That subtile knot, which makes us man:
> So must pure lovers soules descend
>   T'affections, and to faculties,
> Which sense may reach and apprehend,
>   Else a great Prince in prison lies.

That certainly is poetry of a different order. The ghost of hypothesis has been exorcised and we are getting real thought; thought which is both strenuous ('As our blood labours to beget') and finely meticulous ('such fingers need to knit / That subtle knot'). Donne is very much alive to the scrupulous and loving care demanded of him here. It is a classic statement of the wholeness of human experience, but a wholeness – that is its strength – analytically derived. Donne has seen that the impulse that aspires upwards out of material existence is as much an impulse of the blood, as it is of some rarefied spiritual essence, and that it is the meeting of the blood 'aspiring' and the soul 'descending' in desire for embodiment which knits the subtle knot. Much of the criticism I've been directing at the poem falls to the ground here, for the 'great Prince' who lies in prison is the whole self, the whole being who is dependent on the joint activity of 'blood' and 'soule' if he is to take his rightful, bounteous, governing role in the world. Body and soul are therefore dissolved as separate entities, and at their dissolution the elements of role and parody (their 'voices', as it were) also vaporise. The utterance now has a weight and seriousness which is new to the poem. Donne sounds as if he has found his voice and lost his personae.

The pity of it is that the poem which classically creates a meaning for wholeness should revert dismally to its own dichotomies. If the knot is subtle, Donne is subtler, and he proceeds to its unravelling. What had been insight is converted into rationale. Analytic intelligence sets about re-applying its discoveries in the old dualistic terms, justifying what, given 'That subtle knot, which makes us man', needed no justification. 'To'our bodies turne we then.' It is desperately bathetic, and possible only because, even at the heart of the synthesis, there had been a poison of contradiction:

So must pure lovers soules descend.

In its context that ought to mean, 'There is as deep a fittingness in the soul's descending as there was in the blood's aspiring: "As ... So ..." And the soul demonstrates its true purity by accepting that fittingness.' But in the light of the poem's ending, it seems also to mean, 'Bodily life being what it so sordidly is, the soul must compromise its purity by this descent, and its best resource, having done so, is to brazen it out with a stout pretence that nothing has really changed in the process':

> Let him still marke us, he shall see
> Small change, when we'are to bodies gone.

The affectation of undergoing this shameful metamorphosis self-sacrificially, for the benefit of 'Weake men', serves as well as another to conceal the degradation, the *mésalliance* of the soul with the inferior body.

The poem ends, as quoted, on a note of urbane defiance – defiance for which the synthetic union of soul and body has never been anything more than an expedient fiction.

The problem of the proper relation between soul and body, it hardly needs saying, remains as obscure as ever. Donne gropes his way out of the room he has plunged into darkness. Soul is, in a superficial sense, triumphant. Impotent itself, and overweening in its impotence as only conscious purity can be, it has nevertheless forced the body to act out its avid theoretical lusts, preserving its purity by a proxy debauch. Perhaps it's this perverse and barren triumph that makes the dulcet tones of the last quatrain faintly repellent: lilies that fester smell far worse than weeds.

One might expect, after this, to find something sweeter and cleaner about the frankly sensual Donne. Perhaps it was only the intrusion of a spiritualising strain foreign to his nature that produced this unease. Perhaps he was, after all, a good clean weed not a lily, a stout old pagan injuriously thrust into a guilt-ridden and ascetic society where 'late law' was continually chipping away at nature's freedom. That was certainly a view of himself that Donne liked to entertain and upon which, at times, he acted, as a poet. The salient case is 'Elegie 19: Going to Bed'.

It's a poem one comments upon at the risk of commenting much more comprehensively upon oneself and one's inhibitions – but the risk has to be taken. First impressions of the piece are commonly powerful. One comes upon it in late adolescence, and it seems a great and glorious hymn in praise of sexual liberty and discovery, which one treasures accordingly. I don't mean to sneer; it is all that, and movingly so:

> Licence my roaving hands, and let them go,
> Before, behind, between, above, below.
> O my America! my new-found-land,

My kingdome, safeliest when with one man man'd,
My Myne of precious stones, My Emperie,
How blest am I in this discovering thee!

For all the ecstatic exclamatoriness, the feeling does come out clean
and pure and soaring; and if we pause momentarily over the faintly
gloating note of 'Before, behind, between ...' it's only to reproach
ourselves for a kind of inverted prurience, and dismiss the suspicion.

But if the prurience were Donne's ...? And if his way of dealing with
it were to insist all the more on the physicality, forcing himself, and
forcing us to visualise it?

                              ...and though
          Ill spirits walk in white, we easly know,
          By this these Angels from an evil sprite,
          Those set our hairs, but these our flesh upright.

The jest is too shallow to be anything more than an insistence on the
mere mechanics of erection, the second insistence in the poem ('The
foe oft-times having the foe in sight,/Is tir'd with standing though he
never fight' was the first); and it comes, crashingly enough, as part
of an argument for the *sanctity* of these female 'angels'. There is some-
thing related in feeling, perhaps, in the later dwelling upon sexual
posture – 'As liberally, as to a Midwife, shew/Thy self.' Why, in any
case, fasten on a midwife in this context? It takes more skill in modu-
lation than Donne shows in this Elegie to prevent this tonality from
jarring against the note elsewhere of sensual freedom. In the case of the
'upright' flesh there is no modulation at all: we move, without a word
of explanation, from bawdy pun to high celebration. And even when
Donne shows signs of reaching deep into the universal storehouse of
sexual symbol –

          To enter in these bonds, is to be free;
          Then where my hand is set, my seal shall be –

even here, where there is subtle justice done to the element of willing
bondage and irrevocable mutual commitment entailed in such a 'seal-
ing', are we perhaps rather too conscious of the precise location of the
'hand' for the delicate balance of literal and figurative meanings to be
preserved?

This combination of emancipation and self-consciousness generates the theological conceit we have come to expect in these contexts: women

> Themselves are mystick books, which only wee
> (Whom their imputed grace will dignifie)
> Must see reveal'd.

The joke is inoffensive, lightly offered and neatly turned. And yet there is a curious knowingness surrounding the pun-word 'reveal'd' which comes to a head at the startling line 46 (so startling that Grierson, in the teeth of all his own editorial theories, suppressed it) – 'Here is no pennance, much less innocence.' It's not in the least clear whether Donne speaks here for himself or for her; but in either case their emancipated love would appear to be a very seasoned thing indeed. The conclusion follows at once:

> To teach thee, I am naked first; why than
> What needst thou have more covering then a man.

It's still unclear whether we're in the bedroom, or the brothel. The verb 'cover' on which Donne puns belongs to stallions rather than men ('You'll have your daughter cover'd with a Barbary horse,' says Iago to Brabantio) and it imparts a crudity to the final gesture which crowds out the profoundly satisfying sense in which the sexual 'covering' can provide a goodly darkness for the soul and the body. The emancipation in which the poem deals has not quite won its way through to freedom.

And yet – not to be too puritanically graceless – there is something disinterested in Donne's advocacy:

> Full nakedness! All joyes are due to thee,
> As souls unbodied, bodies uncloth'd must be,
> To taste whole joyes.

This is no sophisticated play with religious analogy; it's an attempt to weld sacred and profane into a single reality. Donne doesn't refer the body's joy to the higher joy of the soul for validation; he sees both as 'whole joyes', 'tasted' joys. In this concern for wholeness, 'Going to Bed' stands nearer to religion than all the conscious spirituality of 'The Extasie'. The two poems as a whole share, nevertheless, a certain bad conscience. Risqué theological metaphor is the resort of a man who feels some guilty subservience to the values he nonetheless persists in profaning.

When, in contrast to 'Going to Bed', the relationship is sexually inno-
cent, that too seems to make Donne edgy. It may merely provoke
him to hollow satires like 'Negative Love' which drolly underlines
the inherent superiority of the pure platonic love to all other love
whatsoever – a love which has transcended all desire doesn't know
what it wants, and can never, therefore, be disappointed; or like 'The
Undertaking', which suggests to the man who has achieved heroic
feats of high-minded abstinence, daring to 'forget the Hee and Shee',
that a general knowledge of his exploits may not do much for his
credit: though he has done 'a braver thing/Then all the *Worthies*
did', yet 'a braver thence will spring,/Which is, to keepe that hid'.
These are Donne's neo-platonic riddles and japes.

But 'The Relique', that oddly beautiful and deeply ambiguous
poem, has the same worm of contradiction at its core. The very exis-
tence of the innocently chaste relationship Donne celebrates is what
seems to provoke him to affirm a libertine naturalism, in terms of
which the chastity is completely redundant, even unnatural:

> Difference of sex no more wee knew,
> Then our Guardian Angells doe;
>   Comming and going, wee
> Perchance might kisse, but not between those meales;
>   Our hands ne'r toucht the seales,
> Which nature, injur'd by late law, sets free:
> These miracles wee did...

The man who talks so wisely is not ignorant of 'Difference of sex' –
the patronising worldly reference to 'our Guardian Angells' makes
that plain. Such behaviour was a 'miracle' indeed, but the speaker's
attitude to the miracle is far from clear. There is some suggestion even
that nature's invitation has been foolishly neglected, though there is
equally something right and decent about the neglect, a touching
purity of feeling. Because we are not *told* 'what a miracle shee was',
we are free to speculate whether the palpable admiration he feels –

> but now alas,
> All measure, and all language, I should passe,
> Should I tell what a miracle shee was –

might not be tinged with regret that she wasn't a trifle *less* miracu-
lous, tinged even with a resentment liable to pass 'All measure, and
all language' if given rein.

Quite in what sense nature, 'injur'd by late law', *has* set the seals free, never actually transpires. Much of the utterance and the incidental wit of the poem (e.g. 'For graves have learn'd that womanhead/To be to more then one a Bed') belongs to a world where 'late law' plainly remains injurious to nature's freedom. The tone fluctuates between a tough worldliness ('All women shall adore us, and some men') and a pained, wondering naivety:

> Will he not let'us alone,
> And thinke that there a loving couple lies.

In the end the love wholly evades definition: the worshippers, unlike those of 'The Canonization', provide no credal formulation of the love; they are guilty of 'misdevotion' which makes a mockery of the simple, stark, enigmatic reality:

> A bracelet of bright haire about the bone.

Love's mystery here is genuinely mysterious in its strange amalgam of (so one would have thought) incompatible feelings. For what is this an emblem of? The poignant simplicity of a posthumous love-token? A grisly copulation-symbol? A vision of bright life in the black charnel-house? A deathly tryst to which the poet has been driven by an impossible and beautiful chastity? Who could say? And who could say 'what a miracle *shee* was', especially in view of the unexplained and grating hint that she was a 'Mary Magdalene' and he 'a something else thereby'? I don't think Donne has given us materials for an answer. The enigmatic is of the poem's essence. The knot of feeling persists to the end.

What is beginning to emerge from these readings is a very curious and conscious relation in Donne's poetry between the higher and the lower loves. Each is a reaction, a revulsion from the other, and with neither can Donne make his peace. His sense of the ridiculous punctures the idealisation, and his unquenched thirst for the ideal makes him restless with the merely fleshly. His only hope – and we've seen him grasping it in a few great lyrics – is to realise for himself a love so present that the desperate oscillation of spirit loses itself in the vastness of fulfilment.

This is the ground beyond the personal where conscious objective

and ideal can founder and melt, growing soft and responsive to a
reality indefeasibly outside the self. The ground, ultimately, is nature.
There he is at one with the budding of growing things, with the
'mixt soule' of ordinary human organisms, and with the 'working
vigour' of the sun. This world is the greater circle which contains the
smaller dualistic schema of 'The Extasie' and 'Going to Bed', and
from within which he can watch and comment upon the lovely,
unimaginable springing of his love. And with the acceptance of the
necessary, beautiful impurity of the love, it's as if the crushing load of
an impossible idealism were slipping from his shoulders – or it would
be, if the tone weren't so manifestly that of a man who has always
known, however he played with the fashionable fictions of the higher
love, that the actuality was richer, rooted in earth:

> I scarce beleeve my love to be so pure
>   As I had thought it was,
>   Because it doth endure
> Vicissitude, and season, as the grasse;
> Me thinkes I lyed all winter, when I swore,
> My love was infinite, if spring make'it more.
>
> But if this medicine, love, which cures all sorrow
> With more, not onely bee no quintessence,
> But mixt of all stuffes, paining soule, or sense,
> And of the Sunne his working vigour borrow,
> Love's not so pure, and abstract, as they use
> To say, which have no Mistresse but their Muse,
> But as all else, being elemented too,
> Love sometimes would contemplate, sometimes do.

Which of these Love should be doing at any particular moment is
something only Love can decide. The question is not debated between
the contemplative soul and the 'doing' body. It's a matter of what
Love 'would'; and that, it transpires in the next stanza, is most likely
to be 'Gentle love deeds':

> Gentle love deeds, as blossoms on a bough,
> From loves awakened root do bud out now.

We are not invited to speculate as to *who* awakened love's root. The
question, in any case, answers itself. The root reaches down into the
great substratum where all that is natural – love, sorrow, growth,

pain, 'Vicissitude, and season' – is a part of one Nature, to which humanity is connected profoundly and beyond consciousness.

It would seem rather pointless to enquire whether a love which is rooted here is 'higher' or 'lower'. The fatuity of such distinctions probably needs no further urging. But it's piquant to note that the poem which takes its stand so firmly on the natural, and which is so studied in its neglect of transcendental sanctions, is also the poem which generates one of Donne's most powerful religious metaphors. 'Loves awaken'd root' became, in 1619,

> As the trees sap doth seeke the root below
> In winter, in my winter now I goe,
> Where none but thee, th'Eternall root of true Love I
> may know.

The season has changed. Winter, despite the warm optimism on which 'Loves Growth' ended, *has* abated the spring's increase. But the same great, primal confidence persists, which will allow the rhythms of natural affection to follow their own dark course.

In Donne's best religious poetry there is no shallow antithesis between the natural man and religious man, but a deep continuity.

6

Divinity, Love and Wonder
Holy Sonnets, 'A Litanie', Anniversaries

There's an adage of uncertain origin to which Donne several times refers as if it were so well-known as to need no defence; it runs, 'All love is wonder.' In 'A Valediction: of the booke', the formula is expanded to take in a new term: 'all Divinity/Is love or wonder.' This is thrown off very much in passing, but it's a pregnant sentence nonetheless, and one which says something important about the finest of Donne's religious lyrics. The 'love' there may be of a peculiarly austere kind and the 'wonder' strangely compounded with fear (wonder often is), but the religion that articulates itself in that handful of major poems is very much a matter of those two qualities – and especially of wonder.

Equally, if I had to say in a few words what I believed to be the chief deficiency of the bulk of the *Divine Poems*, I think it would be the *lack* of any sense of wonder that I'd fasten on. When I speak of a lack, of course, I don't mean we go to the poems in search of 'a sense of wonder' and consign them to critical perdition when they fail to supply it; I mean that the poems awaken us to the appropriateness of a response they never themselves begin to rise to, and when one interrogates the vague dissatisfaction they leave, it turns out to be connected with a certain shallow assurance which is the very opposite of wonder.

> Then turne
> O pensive soule, to God, for he knowes best
> Thy true griefe, for he put it in my breast.
>
> ('Holy Sonnet 8')

is the kind of thing I mean. Or perhaps this:

> One short sleepe past, wee wake eternally,
> And death shall be no more; death, thou shalt die.
>
> ('Holy Sonnet 10')

Dissatisfactions more than vague, however, will be propagating if I keep on using the word 'wonder' like a talisman instead of saying what I mean by it. But definition is strictly impossible: wonder in the abstract, wonder which is not in relation, not a wondering *at* something, is not wonder at all but a pursuit of pious gratification – a sanctimonious mummery. The Donne of the worst religious verse is continually exhorting us to wonder of this vacuous kind.

When wonder does come upon a man it has nothing to do with the pursuit of desirable spiritual states. It's more likely to be an involuntary seismic shift occurring so far below the surface of conscious life that the man himself is hardly aware of it – except as a mysterious enlargement of his world. To be as concrete as possible – Tom Brangwen, in *The Rainbow*, is in the grip of this kind of wonder as he drifts towards marriage with Lydia Lensky:

As he worked alone on the land, or sat up with his ewes at lambing time, the facts and material of his daily life fell away, leaving the kernel of his purpose clean. And then it came upon him that he would marry her and she would be his life.

Gradually, even without seeing her, he came to know her. He would have liked to think of her as of something given into his protection, like a child without parents. But it was forbidden him. He had to come down from this pleasant view of the case. She might refuse him. And besides, he was afraid of her.

But during the long February nights with the ewes in labour, looking out from the shelter into the flashing stars, he knew he did not belong to himself. He must admit that he was only fragmentary, something incomplete and subject. There were the stars in the dark heaven travelling, the whole host passing by on some eternal voyage. So he sat small and submissive to the greater ordering.[1]

There are many relations a man can have to his own experience. We are not all – and it's not desirable we should be – Tom Brangwens. What in him is a dignified submission to realities that dwarf his fretful strivings for self-substantiation and autonomy, might in another man (a Donne, say) be a craven flight from a necessary battle in his own soul which he is bound to see through to the end. But for most the bitter end does come, when it seems finally more dignified in a man to admit that the vastnesses he confronts are not to be tamed, and to

[1] *The Rainbow*, ch. I.

acquiesce in his own defeat. Then, 'in the starry multiplicity of the night', wonder comes upon him. Out of that impulse of human dignity – refusing to pretend to command the great travelling hosts – religion is born.

It needn't, of course, be religion in any obvious sense, any more than Brangwen's proposal is 'religious'. The great love lyrics we've been admiring have this kind of calm yet awed openness about them, while remaining splendidly secular. But in the relation Donne chooses to have with his own experience, in his aptness to wonder over it, there are seeds of the religious. And in the case of 'Loves Growth' we have seen one of those seeds germinating.

Religious contemplation of the kind I mean – just to clear it of the last vestiges of pietistic narrowness – is what Wordsworth classically embodies when he is least conscious of being a believer in anything, and has given his mind wholly and absorbedly to the understanding of his past:

> As one who hangs down-bending from the side
> Of a slow-moving boat, upon the breast
> Of a still water, solacing himself
> With such discoveries as his eye can make
> Beneath him in the bottom of the deep,
> Sees many beauteous sights – weeds, fishes, flowers,
> Grots, pebbles, roots of trees, and fancies more,
> Yet often is perplexed and cannot part
> The shadow from the substance, rocks and sky,
> Mountains and clouds, reflected in the depth
> Of the clear flood, from things which there abide
> In their true dwelling; now is crossed by gleam
> Of his own image, by a sunbeam now,
> And wavering motions sent he knows not whence,
> Impediments that make his task more sweet;
> Such pleasant office have we long pursued
> Incumbent o'er the surface of past time...[1]

That beautifully evoked sense of depths within depths, of surfaces which are themselves depths, and the delicate perception that the play of light and image is significant precisely in that it is uninterpretable – this is a way of living with experience which keeps it fresh and

[1] *The Prelude* (1850), IV, 256–72.

sweet, which discovers the significance of things, not by any earnest straining after Meaning, but by eloquent relaxation of attention. The wonder which permeates the passage is partly at the naturalness of it all.

The antithesis of wonder is mystery. Mystery wants to possess its wonder and lock it up in a conceptual box. Mystery offers no release into the Wordsworthian stillness of contemplation; it is tight, self-regarding and aggressive. When all love is not wonder, but mystery, we get poems like 'The Canonization' and 'The Extasie'. When Divinity is mystery, not love or wonder, we get doctrinal gymnastics like 'La Corona' and the majority of the *Holy Sonnets* – poems which know so well in advance what the range of possible feelings is, that they are incapable of feeling any of them.

Donne, of course, in both the erotic and the religious context, insists on the mysteriousness: the insisting is one of the marks that wonder is absent. But the last thing he means by love's mysteriousness (in 'The Canonization') is 'wavering motions sent he knows not whence'; when he tells us (in 'The Extasie') that 'Loves mysteries in soules doe grow', he immediately indicates the work of reference in which we can inform ourselves about the mystery ('But yet the body is his booke'); and when, in 'Holy Sonnet 12', we are enjoined to 'wonder at a greater wonder' (the first wonder having proved rather a damp squib), Donne is at pains to explain exactly what this wonder is, thus effectively preventing our feeling anything more for it than a mild, straying curiosity.

It is a matter, finally, of the attitude you take to what you do not and cannot know. If you want it brought under immediate control, you can call it a mystery, and thus belittle it, tame it. It belongs thereafter to a category of things about which you know the precise extent of your ignorance. No further exertion can be expected of you: it is a mystery. Many of the *Divine Poems* offer us that domesticated unknown – a world in which even the unknown of death can be parcelled up and dispatched:

> Death be not proud, though some have called thee
> Mighty and dreadfull, for, thou art not soe.

No doubt the audacity is deliberate. But is the bland superficiality, as well? It's like nothing so much as the voice of Mr Worldly Wiseman:

'I would advise thee, then, that thou with all speed get thyself rid of thy burden; for thou wilt never be settled in thy mind till then.' These poems may be divine, but they strike me as radically irreligious.

But we are not statutorily confined to the triumphal brassiness of 'Death be not proud'; there are other things, like the deep sonorities of that moving meditation upon death 'A Nocturnall upon S. Lucies day'. There, another impulse, not unlike Lawrence's and Wordsworth's, is at work: an impulse to abandon 'control' in the limited sense and search for some deeper ground of union with that which – however we struggle – still lies beyond us, vastnesses ultimately uncolonisable.

Once the comparison is made, the sonnet, impressive in its own battering way, sinks into proper perspective. You could say that the difference between the two poems is that, for the 'Nocturnall', someone has actually died whereas, for the sonnet, no one has and no one seems likely to. One is a poem about a death; the other a poem about Death whose author, in a manner thoroughly characteristic of 'mystery', seems to think that Death is somehow more important than dying and can be discussed without reference to it. But that's still too shallow a view of the case. The 'Nocturnall' is about more than a death. Momentous though the woman's death is, so momentous that only a quintessence of nothingness survives her, there is something even more momentous to which the catastrophe points – though 'points' is exactly the *wrong* word for the way we are made aware of it.

The state of soul this death has plunged Donne into is one so strange as to stand very nearly outside 'time's covenant'. That is why he is so specific about the time – the once and once only moment at the year's turning. St Lucy's night is his version of Eliot's 'Midwinter spring', the axial instant from which either extinction or renewal might follow, and the man who is exposed to it cannot possibly know which.

> Midwinter spring is its own season
> Sempiternal though sodden towards sundown,
> Suspended in time, between pole and tropic.
> When the short day is brightest, with frost and fire,
> The brief sun flames the ice, on pond and ditches,
> In windless cold that is the heart's heat,

Reflecting in a watery mirror
A glare that is blindness in the early afternoon.
And glow more intense than blaze of branch, or brazier,
Stirs the dumb spirit: no wind, but pentecostal fire
In the dark time of the year. Between melting and freezing
The soul's sap quivers. There is no earth smell
Or smell of living thing. This is the spring time
But not in time's covenant.[1]

At this moment hope or fear, faith or despair are all equally gratuitous.
Whatever it is that is going to happen, will happen. More appallingly,
nothing will ever happen again.

Tis the yeares midnight, and it is the dayes,
Lucies, who scarce seaven houres herself unmaskes,
The Sunne is spent, and now his flasks
Send forth light squibs, no constant rayes;
The worlds whole sap is sunke:
The generall balme th'hydroptique earth hath drunk,
Whither, as to the beds-feet, life is shrunke,
Dead and enterr'd.

And yet even this extremity of unbeing is a rooted thing. That per-
sistent master-metaphor is here too: 'The worlds whole sap is sunke'.
The sense of nothingness phrases itself in terms of seasonal process
and the darkened wintry landscape contains at least one great derelict
tree.

About the *personal* possibility of renewal, though, Donne remains
bitterly, sardonically agnostic:

Study me then, you who shall lovers bee
At the next world, that is, at the next Spring.

There's an immense resource of courage and endurance behind that
note of weary self-mockery, but it does nothing to alter the situation,
'For I am every dead thing' – nothing can change that. Donne there-
fore gives himself up to a lacerating and stony laughter at his own in-
creasing emptiness. The nothing from which he suffers hasn't even
the reality of pain. He lurches from one unfeeling state to another, con-
scious only that he is, if anything, feeling less than the last nothing-
ness:

[1] 'Little Gidding', I, *Four Quartets.*

> From dull privations, and leane emptinesse[1]
> He ruin'd mee, and I am re-begot
> Of absence, darknesse, death; things which are not.

The tragic grotesqueness of it all is unspeakable.

Then, in the dark time of the year, the darkest time of the year, the soul's sap quivers. Donne is suddenly, involuntarily – for there's no sequential, discursive connexion – overtaken and shaken by memory. The dead nerve begins to throb:

> Oft a flood
> Have wee two wept, and so
> Drownd the whole world, us two; oft did we grow
> To be two Chaosses, when we did show
> Care to ought else; and often absences
> Withdrew our soules, and made us carcasses.

Meditating upon 'nothing', Donne has revived the memory of a time when there was something to measure it against, not this relativistic desert of unbeing; and he breaks out in anguish and outrage: 'And we thought *then* that we knew what Nothing was like, poor loving fools that we were! little suspecting in our infantine innocence how much more harrowing a Nothing fate had in store.' But because of the outrage the blackness now holds a tiny spark of human feeling amidst all the inhuman blankness. A new movement is about to begin in the poem.

I call it a movement, though the distance the poem actually travels is infinitesimal. It's the distance between 'Tis the yeares midnight, and it is the dayes' as the *principal* clause, and the subordination of that truth, by the end, to a strange deathly resolution: 'Let mee prepare towards her...*since* this/Both the yeares, and the dayes deep midnight is.' Given the axial nature of this moment in time, though, the infinitesimal is as good as infinite. If just one thing stirs, there will be light again. There will even be 'summer', though not in the foreseeable future, naturally, for the man so narrowly rescued from annihilation. If there is a return for him, it will be slow to the point of imperceptibility. But as his numbed insensibility begins painfully to

---

[1] The colon after 'emptinesse' is editorial and, I think, needless.

thaw, with the admission that there was, once, a 'we', the break comes.

It's the beginning of the fourth stanza. Only now can Donne bring himself to name his grief – '*her* death'. Immediately, from unsuspected depths of the self, comes a solemn rejoinder:

> But I am by her death, (*which word wrongs her*)...

Parenthesis or not, it's an utterly new voice. Something like the unobtrusive entry of an instrument one has not even suspected in the orchestra with a theme that offers authoritatively to clarify all that has gone before. In that plangent stress on the word 'wrongs' lies the dignity of the life that is recovering itself. What is lost irrecoverably must still be valued beyond death. His wrongs are nothing, but there are some wrongs not to be tolerated: one may not speak the 'truths' which wrong that part of her being which remains in his care and keeping. They are not even truths.

It stays, for all that, a parenthesis. As far as the overt argument of the poem goes, nothing has changed. The last two stanzas run in the same channels as the first three: 'I am nothing, nothing, and nothing again!' The whole logical weight descends on the negation, 'But I am None; nor will my Sunne renew.' That is wholly true. But not a whole truth. Perhaps because of the way the voice has calmly assumed *responsibility* for its own nothingness, there is an accumulating momentum, a kind of suppressed excitement of purpose, which is very different from the mocking self-contempt of the opening. And the purpose only authenticates itself further by refusing to become the dominant pulse of the poetry. The spurious consolation would have been noisy in its assertion; the genuine hope will be too much aware of the despair it contends with, to assert anything – or even to be hopeful.

> But I am by her death, (which word wrongs her)
> Of the first nothing, the Elixer grown;
>   Were I a man, that I were one,
>   I needs must know; I should preferre,
>   If I were any beast,
> Some ends, some means; Yea plants, yea stones detest,
> And love; All, all some properties invest;
> If I an ordinary nothing were,
> As shadow, a light, and body must be here.

> But I am None; nor will my Sunne renew.
> You lovers, for whose sake, the lesser Sunne
>   At this time to the Goat is runne
>   To fetch new lust, and give it you,
>   Enjoy your summer all;
> Since shee enjoyes her long nights festivall,
> Let mee prepare towards her, and let mee call
> This houre her Vigill, and her Eve, since this
> Both the yeares, and the dayes deep midnight is.

A return to the opening, yes. But it's one of those recapitulations which make us aware of the immense distance travelled since the words were first spoken. They had a purport then, but their significance had not emerged. To invoke the 'Little Gidding' experience again:

>   what you thought you came for
> Is only a shell, a husk of meaning
> From which the purpose breaks only when it is fulfilled
> If at all. Either you had no purpose
> Or the purpose is beyond the end you figured
> And is altered in fulfilment.

Donne is discovering what he had not known, but has meant all along. The alternation in fulfilment is registered unobtrusively in the added adjective, 'deep': the midnight has indeed become 'deep'.

But what is it that Donne resolves to do, in the last lines? It's impossible to say, except in his own phrase 'prepare towards her'. It sounds like someone untwisting the last strands of man in himself and giving way to despair. Suicide, ultimately. There is no reason offered for regarding the unutterable blankness and silence as 'her long nights *festivall*', not for calling his unhoping, hopeless watch, a 'Vigill' – which would be the devout man's preparation for a feast-day. Whatever sense of renewed possibility we find in these gestures – and it's impossible not to feel some – we find it on our own responsibility. But precisely because Donne does not break up his lines to weep with joy and relief, we are convinced that the possibility of some extraordinary gaiety transfiguring all that dread, some unimaginable jubilance, has veritably come upon him. Come upon him at a moment of profane and mocking hopelessness – 'Enjoy your summer all' – and transformed the bitter capitulation into an act of religious concentration: 'Let mee prepare towards her.' The religion is, of course, indistinguishable from the human love it honours.

Strikingly, the reason offered for that 'preparation' is simply that it *is* deep midnight. That is to say, the logic of feeling implied by 'since' is no earthly logic: if anything follows from the totality of darkness, it would be the consummate pointlessness of preparing towards anything. Yet, by a paradox of feeling which we'll meet again ('Churches are best for Prayer, that have least light'), the soul finds its freedom precisely in that spiritual vacuum. Because it need not feel or do anything ever again, it discovers that it can and does feel and act.

I've talked at length about a poem from the *Songs and Sonets* in a chapter on the *Divine Poems* because I want to recover for the word 'religious' a meaning which is badly served by the standard divisions in the collected Donne. Also, because I would like it to be clear that, if I am, on the whole, wearied by the *Holy Sonnets,* that is because I am deeply impressed by something incompatible. With the 'Nocturnall' firmly in mind, one should avoid becoming querulous about lesser things.

And yet the querulousness arises because of an irritant in the sonnets themselves, an annoying contradiction of feeling. On the one hand they are *jeux*, products of wit in its limited modern sense – as a persistent strain of logical playfulness makes clear:

> From rest and sleepe, which but thy [Death's] pictures bee,
> Much pleasure, then from thee, much more must flow.
>
> ('Holy Sonnet 10')

Or

> Thy lawes abridgement, and thy last command
> Is all but love; Oh let this last Will stand!
>
> ('Holy Sonnet 16')

It's analogous to the playful exuberance which permits Donne cheerily to station the trumpeters of the Last Judgment 'At the round earths *imagin'd* corners', thus showing himself considerably more imbued with the spirit of Copernicus than that of John of Patmos (cf. his sprightliness with 'And the angel took the censer and filled it with fire of the altar and cast it into the earth: and there were voices, and

thunderings, and lightnings, and an earthquake. And the seven
angels which had the seven trumpets prepared themselves to sound' –
Revelation, vii, 5–6).

This mode would present no problems in itself: it would simply
convey an unabashed and rather taking vivacity, in the face of terrors
over which other people insist on growing gloomy. But on the other
hand, when you consider the pitch and timbre of the *Holy Sonnets* as a
whole, it's impossible not to feel that they either dispense, or would
like to dispense, more than a little gloom themselves; and that their
author would have been offended at anyone who refused to take them
seriously – more seriously, indeed, than he himself seems prepared to
do. The reader, consequently, is always getting caught out with an
ill-timed smirk on his face; or alternatively, plunged into sombre
meditation in deference to the poet's earnestness, he becomes irritat-
ingly aware that the mercurial gentleman is now disposed to be
merry. This rapid oscillation of feeling – a kind of uncontrolled ironic
tic – has the effect of prompting reflections not altogether reassuring
upon the stability of the faith the poetry proffers us, and misgivings
about the impulse that is carrying Donne towards religion.

Now obviously, this thought and these misgivings had occurred to
a man who agonised for years over his decision to enter the priest-
hood, and he would be an indelicate commentator who would offer to
pronounce upon the justice of that decision. Nevertheless, if it is true
that, as I've argued, it contributes to Donne's greatness as a poet that
he is prepared to let his idiosyncrasies of mind and feeling work them-
selves out in their own way, one is bound to take note, in the *Divine
Poems*, of a studious attempt to repress the idiosyncratic, and an effort,
sometimes very visible, to bend an individualist temper to bear the
yoke of a common faith. The poetic effect, as might have been pre-
dicted, is often to give us the idiosyncratic, oddly distorted by the
strains of self-abasement, wreathed in strange distracting shapes
around the familiar doctrines – like a serpent round a crucifix. The
most palpable case is 'La Corona', where the serpent is doubly
distracting in that he appears to believe himself invisible.

A good deal of light was shed on this strenuous pursuit of anony-
mity by Coleridge, when he very pregnantly related a certain willed
austerity in the religious verse, to the 'opulence' of the secular verse.
(The commentary is 'biographical' in the richest and most tactful

way: it explores, in terms of a particular life, the life one feels fitfully and somewhat abortively stirring in the verse.) The austerity and the opulence are not, he proposes, antithetical: the one is not the moral corrective applied to the excesses of the other. On the contrary, they both proceed from the same Donne-like 'pride in doing what he likes with his own':

The will-worship, in squandering golden hecatombs on a Fetisch, on the first stick or straw met with at rising – this pride of doing what he likes with his own, fearless of an immense surplus to pay all lawful debts...this is Donne! He was an orthodox Christian only because he could have been an infidel *more* easily; and, therefore willed to be a Christian: and he was a Protestant, because it enabled him to lash about to the right and to the left, and without a *motive*, to say better things for the Papists than they could say for themselves. It was the impulse of a purse-proud opulence of innate power![1]

Grant the plausibility of this reconstruction and a number of things become intelligible. One can see why the self-abnegation of the *Divine Poems* should frequently remain less chastened than baroque, in both its temper and its ornament; why the temptations to infidelity, which are evidently omnipresent, should be so rarely met at any other level than that of a rather hectic drama. And one can see why an exercise like 'A Litanie' should be uniformly unconvincing in its attempts to simulate the offering of a devotional consensus: the weighty impersonality of true liturgical utterance is simply not available to a man who could '*more* easily' have been an infidel, and the stanzas that attempt it never rise above the ingenious, the ornate or the curious. The verse comes to life only as Donne reckons with the very personal strains he feels in being a believer at all. It's no use his pretending, one is tempted to exclaim, that the yoke of religion is easy and its burden light: for him it is not.

> That wee may change to evennesse
> This intermitting aguish Pietie;
> That snatching cramps of wickednesse
> And Apoplexies of fast sin, may die;
> That musique of thy promises,
> Not threats in Thunder may
> Awaken us to our just offices...
> ...Lord heare us, when wee pray.

[1] R. F. Brinkley (ed.), *Coleridge on the Seventeenth Century* (1955), p. 523.

And yet the reckoning with those personal strains may also set the reader questioning further their intensity and extent. For doesn't one detect a slight, and irrelevant skittishness here ('snatching cramps of wickednesse', indeed!), as if the witty Donne were aware of some lingering attachment to the elements in himself which *made* his piety intermitting and aguish, and of a residual repugnance to 'evennesse'? It is true, one can read parts of 'A Litanie' as Donne's weighing and paradoxical balancing of the two opposing strains in himself; and then he is impressive:

> From being anxious, or secure,
> Dead clods of sadnesse, or light squibs of mirth,
> From thinking, that great courts immure
> All, or no happinesse, or that this earth
> Is only for our prison fram'd,
> Or that thou art covetous
> To them whom thou lovest, or that they are maim'd
> From reaching this worlds sweet, who seek thee thus,
> With all their might, Good Lord deliver us.

That voice has earned its steadiness by a self-scrutiny at once sober and energetic. But neither the steadiness nor the self-knowledge is much in evidence in the *Holy Sonnets*, though most of them are contemporaneous.

The most usual note, there, is one of moral exertion, Donne 'willing to be a Christian', forcing himself to a contemplation of the Last Things, forcing himself to see as love what he depicts as fear and violation. Forcing it is –

> Wilt thou love God, as he thee! then digest,
> My Soule, this wholsome meditation...
>
> Spit in my face you Jewes, and pierce my side,
> Buffet, and scoffe, scourge, and crucifie mee...
>
> Batter my heart, three person'd God...

And fear – a vision of appalling and eternal reproach –

> Blood fills his frownes, which from his pierc'd head fell...

And violation –

> for I
> Except you'enthrall mee, neer shall be free,
> Nor ever chast, except you ravish mee.

The violence of sentiment in the *Holy Sonnets* springs from the attempt to bend a stubborn temper to something which is seen, from a position *outside* the stubbornness, as a good, a pure good. This view of the case commits Donne immediately to repressive violence: the personality becomes the prey of inner division, because only the consenting, and therefore 'higher' faculties of perception are given any credence; the others, being rebellious, are 'lower'. It's the old, old dualism in a not very new guise.

The Good, in the name of which all this mischief is set working, the Good conceived as existing outside the conflict, finds no convincing poetic expression. It only enters the poetry when there is a question to be begged (as in a phrase like '*holy* discontent', in 'Sonnet 3') or an exercise to be recommended:

> Oh make thy selfe with holy mourning blacke,
> And red with blushing, as thou art with sinne.
>
> ('Sonnet 4')

When the will *knows* what it must persuade to, what it is to will, the process of urging that preconcept is necessarily rhetorical. One is very conscious of structure, organisation, device. Arguments, images, dramatic speech are not ways of uncovering, or exploring, or testing a meaning; they are ways of enforcing it. So that there can be no imaginative commerce, no mutual modification, no fusion of the two components in a conceit or an image – the 'mourning' is so 'holy' it ceases to be mourning: 'holy' likewise subsumes 'discontent', which is allowed no weight at all, but simply swallowed whole by its voracious qualifier; the 'fiery zeale...which doth in eating heale' ('Sonnet 5') is a healing zeal and we ignore the fiery eating; Christ's spouse, who is 'most trew...When she'is embrac'd and open to most men' ('Sonnet 18') is not to be suspected of promiscuity: the paradox is merely gratuitous. The basic poetic activity is what the rhetoricians call 'amplification' of a given truth. The truth is a mystery:

> 'Twas much, that man was made like God before,
> But, that God should be made like man, much more.
>
> ('Sonnet 15')

One can tell it is a mystery because it has been made, by rhetorical means, to seem improbable. But of wonder there is nothing left, and when Donne exhorts us to 'wonder at a greater wonder' ('Sonnet 12') it is because he knows it.

The recommended objects of wonder, handled in this mechanical way, can only be postulates, whose meaningfulness remains in question as long as their propounder is willing to use such questionable methods to recommend them. Does he really mean what he says? Or does he only mean to mean it?

Donne's problem over his own seriousness is, I believe, partly an historical matter. He is reaching for simplicities no longer available to him, or to his age; and to the extent that he succeeds in laying hold on them he must become dubious about their relevance, for they belong to some other language which he cannot make his own:

> I am thy sonne, made with thy selfe to shine,
> Thy servant, whose paines thou hast still repaid,
> Thy sheepe, thine Image, and, till I betray'd
> My selfe, a temple of thy Spirit divine.
>
> ('Sonnet 2')

It's all impeccably orthodox, paraphrased from the purest Scriptural sources – and it reads as paraphrase and nothing more.

Each age has its own special authenticities of faith. Dunbar, in the late fifteenth century, could exult in the destruction of death as if the assurances of Christian dogma were the veriest marketplace truisms, common wisdom upon which the mind could rest with complete certainty. And the certainty pervades the poetry:

> Done is a battell on the dragon blak,
> Our campioun Chryst confountet hes his force;
> The yettis of hell ar brokin with a crak,
> The signe triumphall rasit is of the croce,
> The divillis trymmillis with hiddous voce,
> The saulis ar borrowit and to the blis can go,
> Chryst with his blud our ransonis dois indoce:
> *Surrexit dominus de sepulchro.*

As a state of feeling that is utterly convincing. And convincing in the utterance because Dunbar's language, even at its most abstract, deals in substance not figure; and when it is rhetorical, as it splendidly is, it is rhetorical with a resonance that is wholly *within* the words. One does not ask for the credentials of a man who says with this air of demonstrative finality, '*Done* is a battell on the dragon blak.'

When Donne attempts the same kind of persuasiveness, one is very conscious of rhetorical strain. He is trying to coerce, not celebrating in public language the unquestionable and the assured. So he relies upon a kind of verbal assault and battery which doesn't so much share the language with the reader, as use it as a weapon for the reader's subduing. And one is very conscious, too, of figure. Dunbar can hardly be said to personify at all; he talks about the objective 'dragon blak' and the visible 'yettis of hell'. Donne's personification of death is a blatant device, aimed at cutting death down to size, and the crisp cross-talk of quip and witticism indicates how well he knows he can't really get away with it.

> Death be not proud, though some have called thee
> Mighty and dreadfull, for, thou art not soe,
> For, those, whom thou think'st, thou dost overthrow,
> Die not, poore death, nor yet canst thou kill mee.
> From rest and sleepe, which but thy pictures bee,
> Much pleasure, then from thee, much more must flow,
> And soonest our best men with thee doe goe,
> Rest of their bones, and soules deliverie.

There for a moment Donne touches real conviction, a position from which he can contemplate death harmoniously both as a delivery of the imprisoned soul and a birth into life – but conviction most unlike Dunbar's in its subtle awareness of the double aspect of things.

A blustering sophistry supervenes:

> Thou art slave to Fate, Chance, kings, and desperate men,
> And dost with poyson, warre, and sicknesse dwell,
> And poppie, or charmes can make us sleepe as well,
> And better then thy stroake; why swell'st thou then?
> One short sleepe past, wee wake eternally,
> And death shall be no more; death, thou shalt die.

It may of course have been Donne's *intention* to carry off the whole affair with a kind of swaggering bravura, as a demonstration of his own freedom from rank superstition and craven fear. If so, it's an intention about whose realisation it's hard to get very excited. To deliberately confound the doctrine of the soul's immortality with the

unconsolingly tautological sense in which Death is 'dead' for the
individual once he has died, as if that were some kind of answer to the
fear of death – it simply indicates how superficially that fear is present
in the poem in the first place. It is paraded like a captive slave and
publicly routed, but it is never met on the level where it really presses.
The destructive possibility that Dunbar figures in those gates of hell
'brokin with a crak' or in those devils that 'trymmillis with hiddous
voce' is much more 'mighty and dreadfull' than the cardboard ogre
Donne engages in mock combat. It is a mock battle partly because
Donne has tried to behave as if the eloquent simplicity of Dunbar's
manner were still available to him when, in truth, a hundred years of
history and his own complex nature had put such a manner per-
manently out of reach.

God is not, could not be, for Donne, a fixed point of reference. For
one thing a century of post-reformation disputation had fragmented
the way of salvation that utters itself with such dignity in Dunbar, or
in a play like *Everyman*. The Protestant could not be so sure of grace
as Everyman had been:

> O glorious fountain, that all uncleanness doth clarify,
> Wash from me the spots of vice unclean,
> That on me no sin may be seen.

Instead of that simple integrity, we have Donne's 'Blacke Soule'
('Sonnet 4'):

> Thou art like a pilgrim, which abroad hath done
> Treason, and durst not turne to whence hee is fled,
> Or like a thiefe, which till deaths doome be read,
> Wisheth himselfe delivered from prison;
> But damn'd and hal'd to execution,
> Wisheth that still he might be imprisoned.
> Yet grace, if thou repent, thou canst not lacke;
> But who shall give thee that grace to beginne?

That is a very ugly predicament. Condemnation is inevitable. The
alternatives are prison and execution. Man is utterly dependent on
grace which is outside himself, yet is responsible for its initiation. The
maddening and frightening circularity is well caught in the verse. But
when Donne tries to apply the traditional salve to his wounded
spirit, his mind won't make meaning of the doctrines he appeals to:

> Oh make thy selfe with holy mourning blacke,
> And red with blushing, as thou art with sinne;
> Or wash thee in Christs blood, which hath this might
> That being red, it dyes red soules to white.

Even if one succeeds in skating over the surface of the cliché about washing in Christ's blood (its functioning depends upon our *not* imagining a 'washing' taking place at all, or it is absurd), the verbal games with colour-symbolism turn the drama of redemption into the antics of a moral chameleon. Such frivolities – however seriously offered – have nothing to say to the sense of necessary and inexorable guilt which is the poem's point of departure.

There's the same frightening inadequacy in the dogma invoked in 'Sonnet 6' ('This is my playes last scene') as a palliative to the fear, not merely of 'gluttonous death' which 'will instantly unjoynt / My body, and soule...', but of God himself:

> But my'ever-waking part shall see that face,
> Whose feare already shakes my every joynt...

All Donne has to shore against the ruins of his self-possession here, is a blatant theological sophistry which we find annotated in the best editions, but which plainly does no more than dramatise his logical bankruptcy:

> Then, as my soule, to'heaven her first seate, takes flight,
> And earth-borne body, in the earth shall dwell,
> So, fall my sinnes, that all may have their right,
> To where they'are bred, and would presse me, to hell.

Another of the meditations on the Last Things, 'Sonnet 13' ('What if this present'), repeats the pattern: the solvent will not dissolve; the consolation does not console.

In each of these cases (Sonnets 4, 6 and 13) the spiritual malady so obviously won't give way to the patent medicine applied to it, that it seems almost to be a part of the poetic strategy to make us aware of this fact. We are to exclaim in mingled awe, horror and sympathy, 'That will not serve! His case is much worse than he knows.' Which leads one further to suspect that the horror is ever so slightly relished for the drama it puts into life: 'valiantly I hels wide mouth o're stride' – there's some gusty self-satisfaction at being caught in that posture.

Perhaps the 'frightening' inadequacy in the consoling dogmas is more what we are *meant* to think, than the result of any created terror in the poetry. Donne is cultivating an image of himself as heroic victim. Is that why, in the most violent of the *Holy Sonnets*, his union with God – a relation in which he cannot be the victim – is nevertheless figured as a rape?

It's a very strange state of feeling we are initiated into in 'Sonnet 14':

> Batter my heart, three person'd God; for, you
> As yet but knocke, breathe, shine, and seeke to mend;
> That I may rise, and stand, o'erthrow mee,'and bend
> Your force, to breake, blowe, burn and make me new.

The poem ends on a conscious note of sweet female passivity. But how is that related to this invocation of violence at the beginning, to the desire to be battered and hammered, overthrown and bent, hurled about with exciting brutality? The compound includes a hankering for *sexual* violence too; and if we want to see that strain as a normal manifestation of an ancient metaphor (the Divine Lover), some explanation has to be offered for Donne's insistently circumstantial handling of it:

> I, like an unsurpt towne, to'another due,
> Labour to'admit you, but Oh, to no end.

(If Donne is merely 'continuing the metaphor of the siege' the breath-less, exclamatory 'but Oh' is inexplicable.) I may be squeamish, but I find that, as addressed to God, cheaply shocking; and the cheapness is not mitigated when, in the immediately succeeding lines, Donne is able to drop with perfect ease into the offhandedly factual tone of a military despatch. The verse is scarcely even competent:

> Reason your viceroy in mee, mee should defend,
> But is captiv'd, and proves weake or untrue.

Quite why God needs to be informed that Reason is His viceroy, or why Donne is so vague about the cause of Reason's defection (weak? or untrue?), or why he has so painfully to explain 'what is happening' – these are questions best left unasked.

> Yet dearely'I love you,'and would be loved faine,
> But am betroth'd unto your enemie.

Language performs its minimal function here – to convey information and nothing else. These are the fumblings of ineffable banality.

And yet in the final quatrain there is a return to the torment and fascination of the basic sexual metaphor, as the battering insensitivity of this God's forced entry is both invoked and rhythmically enacted. The tumbled passionate utterance suggests real, panic ecstasy, and a horrible rapt absorption in the violation that is about to be undergone:

> Divorce mee,'untie, or breake that knot againe,
> Take me to you, imprison mee, for I
> Except you'enthrall mee, never shall be free,
> Nor ever chast, except you ravish mee.

I make no apology for the vulgarity of my reading: the vulgarity is Donne's. And it springs from a dangerously uncontrolled sensationalism which is, all the same, insensible to the sensations it invokes. As in many of the *Holy Sonnets*, there's something hysterically out of control.

And yet, on another level, as with hysteria, it's only too well under control. In a queer way – queer when you think about the alleged subject – the sonnet has a kind of knockabout vitality, as if the whole affair had been staged and could be enjoyed on that level. For all the intimacy of its matter, the manner is inescapably public: fortissimo throughout, with very little you would want to call a nuance. It sounds as if God is at the other end of a public address system in an empty stadium. One finishes up wondering simultaneously whether the forces let loose in the poem aren't too powerful for the kind of ordering that is brought to bear on them; and whether the placid publicity of that ordering doesn't betray a fundamental lack of seriousness about the threat the poem claims to confront.

Both could be true. Where there is no wonder, no natural and internal principle of order in the soul ('Love,' one remembers, 'all love of other sights *controules*'), the mind can only veer wildly from the extremity of self-abandon to the rigours of self-discipline and self-abasement. Both are factitious: the control because it is born of a fear of abandon, and the abandon because it is born of resentment at the control. Action and reaction, with nothing at the centre. But it is a travesty of abandon, anyway, this imperious demand for ravishment. It is so fiercely willed that it destroys the possibility of its own fulfilment. The mind determined to possess the experience of abandonment cannot give itself up to it. And so the encounter with the unknown, which might have flooded the mind with a sudden, impersonal astonishment, pales and vanishes in the hard glare of over-exposed consciousness. The stage has been set in such a way that the drama cannot take place.

On the whole one feels easier with those among the *Holy Sonnets* which don't even arouse expectations of a genuinely religious encounter. Those which are content to inhabit their public realm and, if they embark upon feeling, do so in a decently conventional way. Pieces like 'Sonnet 7: At the round earths imagin'd corners'. This sonnet *is* public, in very much the way of 'Batter my heart', but with much more appropriateness to its subject – the general Resurrection. The manner works well for the first eight lines, with their spine-tingling blaze of brass orchestration. A very fine *Dies Irae*:

> At the round earths imagin'd corners, blow
> Your trumpets, Angells, and arise, arise
> From death, you numberlesse infinities
> Of soules, and to you scattred bodies goe,
> All whom the flood did, and fire shall o'erthrow,
> All whom warre, dearth, age, agues, tyrannies,
> Despaire, law, chance, hath slaine, and you whose eyes,
> Shall behold God, and never tast deaths woe.

The musical analogy forces itself on you; and especially when we get the *forte-piano* entry into the sestet, a sudden huge drop in volume and the emergence of a new penitential strain, very eloquently modulated into a plaintive minor.

> But let them sleepe, Lord, and mee mourne a space,
> For, if above all these, my sinnes abound,
> 'Tis late to aske abundance of thy grace,
> When wee are there; here on this lowly ground,
> Teach mee how to repent; for that's as good
> As if thou'hadst seal'd my pardon, with thy blood.

But if we're talking in musical terms – it's Verdi's *Requiem* that comes to mind, isn't it, rather than Mozart's? The cast of both the apocalyptic terror and the penitential grief is operatic; and the transition from one to the other gives itself away precisely because it is so *effective*. If I can cling to the analogy for a moment, the case of Mozart is very pertinent. Because when he turns, from contemplating the Day of Wrath, to a penitential prayer to be remembered in that day, the musical experience given us is exactly what is missing from Donne's 'effectiveness'. One feels the reflecting mind turning away from all the huge and momentous drama, seeking inwardly for collectedness and composure. And because there are no dramatic and shallow juxtaposings of the *Rex tremendae majestatis* of the Day of Wrath, with the *Jesu pie* of penitence, but only an eloquent and natural movement in upon the self, the terror and the penitence fuse together into a new third thing – a religiousness that grows spontaneously out of the natural man. Religion, in Donne's sonnet, feels like something made.

Which is perhaps why he can afford to be so chirpy about 'the round earths imagin'd corners', can permit himself witty asides about the extraordinary similarity between 'agues' and 'tyrannies', or the capacity of 'law' for slaying as many unwitting victims as 'Despaire' or 'chance'. The sprightliness is very taking, decidedly preferable to the prostration of some of the other 'Doomsday' sonnets; but then, are we also expected to believe that 'above all these, my sinnes abound'? That sounds rather complacently pious – related in feeling to the obligatory long-faces people put on in church-porches as they adjust their head-gear. And although it is, as I've said, decently conventional enough not to jar very badly, it can't be said to offer much for our understanding of what it means to 'behold God' – unless that, too, is a conventional act. For Donne it appears that it is. His God is so much a part of the known worldt hat the ways to Him are also perfectly 'known':

> Teach mee how to repent; for that's as good
> As if thou'hadst seal'd my pardon, with thy blood.

It seems a comfortable enough world to inhabit.

I imagine that Donne's assent could have been secured for most of the grounds on which I've been censuring the *Holy Sonnets* – if not at the time, certainly a few years later. The evidence of the Sermons suggests that he was, consciously at least, as concerned as anybody that mystery should not supplant wonder in religion. The 'consciously', however, is the rub. It is mystery's last bolting-hole, and one down which Donne can be very plainly observed disappearing, in the *Anniversaries*. The strategy is for mystery to set itself up as the apologist of wonder, the approved champion of the unknowable, bustling about importantly and organising our affections into a proper hierarchy, with the Unknown at its apex:

> nothing
> Is worth our travaile, griefe, or perishing
> But those rich joyes, which did possesse her heart,
> Of which she's now partaker, and a part.
>
> ('The first Anniversary', 431–4)

It would be amusing, if it weren't rather depressing – the bland ease of manner and the rhythms of perfect lassitude in which everything earthly is dismissed airily with a wave of the hand.

> Shee, shee is gone; she is gone; when thou knowest this,
> What fragmentary rubbidge this world is
> Thou knowest, and that it is not worth a thought;
> He honors it too much that thinkes it nought.
>
> ('The second Anniversary', 81–3)

By a hollow simulation of the 'Nocturnall''s despairing grief, mystery hopes to qualify as religious. But in order to despair, one needs to have hoped, to have held something in honour, and to be haunted still by the love which a bitter reality conspires to annul. The author of the *Anniversaries* – who must be presumed to stand in a very odd relation to the historical Donne – has no such legacy of broken ideals.

> Forget this rotten world; And unto thee
> Let thine owne times as an old storie bee.
> Be not concern'd: studie not why, nor when;
> Doe not so much as not beleeve a man.
> For though to erre, be worst, to try truths forth,
> Is far more businesse, then this world is worth.
>
> ('The second Anniversary', 49–54)

It is a lethargic pyrrhonism trying to pass itself off as the wondering agnosticism which is the soul of religion. But that-which-we-do-not-know is not a dispenser of exhaustion and lethargy; it's the spring (to quote Hopkins) of 'a dearest freshness deep down things', a guarantee that, however much we colonise and industrialise our mental worlds, 'for all this, nature is never spent'. The claim here to know what 'this world is worth' discounts itself by its own failure of vital energy. The verse comes in little, exhausted spurts, the movement of a mind wading feebly through the tepid shallows of its own torpor. It's plainly the reflex of boredom, bored even with itself. The proper answer to it comes from the younger Donne of 'Satyre 3', and comes in a voice which is as alive with gamesome adventureousness as this voice was toneless with inanition:

> doubt wisely; in strange way
> To stand inquiring right, is not to stray;
> To sleepe, or runne wrong, is. On a huge hill,
> Cragged, and steep, Truth stands, and hee that will
> Reach her, about must, and about must goe;
> And what the hills suddennes resists, winne so...

But 'The second Anniversary' drags its slow length along. By way of explaining its hopeless abandonment of the labour of 'trying truths forth', we are given a token account of the vanity of arts and sciences. What it seems chiefly to suggest (and again the falsification of what we know Donne to have been is baffling) is that the 'labour' has never begun. The stock-in-trade dissatisfactions with human learning, which sceptics and cynics of all ages have wheeled out, make a tired appearance; the mutability of opinion is demonstrated yet again; and a few paradoxes and problems are produced to dash the pride of the natural scientists. Like that arch-pyrrhonist, Doctor Faustus of Wittenberg, Donne records a process of 'education' which has been a progress in disillusion. Some of the exasperation with petty pedants infects the verse, and puts a bit of momentary animation into it; but Donne, unlike Faustus, seems never to have taken his pedants seriously and has correspondingly less ground for grievance:

> Wee see in Authors, too stiffe to recant,
> A hundred controversies of an Ant;
> And yet one watches, starves, freeses, and sweats,
> To know but Catechismes and Alphabets
> Of unconcerning things, matters of fact;
> What *Caesar* did, yea, and what *Cicero* said.
> Why grasse is greene, or why our blood is red,
> Are mysteries which none have reach'd unto.
> ('The second Anniversary', 281–9)

This is sound enough, in its blunt, sensible way. But instead of putting away the silly volume of pedantic ant-lore (you can still see it in the library of Chichester Cathedral, with Donne's name in the fly-leaf), Donne erects upon this foundation of human folly a wholly unwarrantable structure of divine wisdom, which has no more cogency than that it is the exact reverse of everything unsatisfactory in human knowledge. Poor old 'sense', the eternal scapegoat, gets the blame for everything the wit of man has, over the centuries, done amiss:

> When wilt thou shake off this Pedantery,
> Of being taught by sense, and Fantasie?
> Thou look'st through spectacles; small things seeme great
> Below; But up unto the watch-towre get,
> And see all things despoyl'd of fallacies:
> Thou shalt not peepe through lattices of eyes,
> Nor heare through Labyrinths of eares, nor learne
> By circuit, or collections to discerne.
> In heaven thou straight know'st all, concerning it,
> And what concernes it not, shalt straight forget.

One could wish this bold conquistador of the undiscovered country to take a little more interest in 'what concernes it not' – if only because 'what concernes it not' provides the only possible basis for defining 'it'. But the very metaphor Donne uses to establish his heavenly knowledge, portrays it as equally probably a fallacy: the things one sees from the watch-tower may seem as fallaciously small as the small things seemed fallaciously great below. Heaven, on this showing, is a region where the laws of natural perspective no longer obtain – which is what sceptics throughout history have only too shrewdly suspected.

Again Donne is best answered from his own mouth:

Saul was struck blinde, but it was a blindnesse contracted from light... This blindnesse which we speak of which is a sober and temperate abstinence from the immoderate study and curious knowledge of this world, this holy simplicity of the soule, is not a darknesse, a dimnesse, a stupidity in the understanding, contracted by living in a corner, it is not an idle retiring into a Monastery, or into a Village, or a Country solitude, it is not a lazy affectation of ignorance; not darknesse, but a greater light, must make us blinde.

(*Sermons*, VI, 215 – 30 January 1624/5)

The *Anniversaries* most conspicuously lack any 'greater light', though they have more than their share of the darkness of wilful obfuscation.

Their meditation on the uncertainty of human knowledge doesn't open out upon a larger space for human freedom. It lacks that kind of disinterestedness: the meditation is itself constrictingly and repressively pedantic. The aim seems much more to belittle the known world than to propose any other. There is no breathing space here for 'this holy simplicity of soule' of which the Sermon speaks. The soul is condemned to inhabit a dead universe the mind has made, in which 'nothing/Is worth our travaile, griefe, or perishing'.

There is one of the Sonnets, though, which marvellously achieves that difficult simplicity, and this takes us to the threshold, chronologically and poetically, of the *Hymnes*. It is later than most of the other Sonnets, by about eight years, and again the occasion is a death – his wife's.

If the prevailing manner of the other Sonnets was operatic – emotion scored for large orchestra – this is unaccompanied song, sparse, ardent and deeply expressive – a kind of shaped self-communing. Donne is looking deeply into the waters of his experience and attempting the delicate task of parting shadow from substance:

> Since she whome I lovd, hath payd her last debt
> To Nature, and to hers, and my good is dead
> And her soule early into heaven ravished,
> Wholy in heavenly things my mind is sett.
> Here the admyring her my mind did whett
> To seeke thee God; so streames do shew the head,
> But though I have found thee, and thou my thirst hast fed,
> A holy thirsty dropsy melts mee yett.
> But why should I begg more love, when as thou
> Dost wooe my soule for hers; offring all thine:
> And dost not only feare least I allow
> My love to saints and Angels things divine
> But in thy tender jealosy dost doubt
> Least the World, fleshe, yea Devill putt thee out.
>
> ('Holy Sonnet 17'[1])

As with all living things, the source of the poem's life can't be precisely located: one senses it in the extraordinarily expressive un-rhythms of the opening, the fall of stress continually checked by some

---

[1] I follow the text of the Westmoreland MS, of which all the edited versions are sophistications, and possibly misleading ones.

scruple which it takes the whole poem, and more, to articulate; one senses it in the subdued play on the word 'ravished' – a pun which, in 'Batter my heart', had been the last stunt in a spiritual spectacular, but which here beautifully balances the accusations against, and the submission to God. It's there, too, in all the schematic connexions Donne doesn't make, in the consoling conclusion he does not arrive at, and in the paramount question he fails to answer – 'But why should I begg more love?' The delicate probing of motive and emotion works all around that organic trouble spot, but seems finally to think it best not to interfere with the natural healing processes.

So the question lingers on. Though the poem is suffused with a great warmth of feeling, both for the dead woman and for God, there is also an incompleteness: 'But though I have found thee, and thou my thirst hast fed ... my thirst is not fed: a holy thirsty dropsy melts me yet. It is my disease. I do not pretend to justify it. Now that I have found the head of the stream which flowed in her admired life, I must be content. It cannot be otherwise. But I am not. And isn't my disease, which melts me in desire and love, as holy as it is immoderately thirsty? Why should I beg more love? I don't know. But I do. And you must know it is inevitable.' It is a great and courageous candour that can so calmly lay itself bare; though it expects, one notes, an equal candour from God, as the naked directness of address reveals – 'To seeke thee God' – not 'O Lord', or 'deare Christ', or 'three-person'd God', but 'thee God'.

It's a part of that candour that a whole series of stock reactions and connexions are passed by as if they didn't – as indeed they don't – exist. Donne does not feel that, if he believes her soul is 'in heaven', his 'good' is any the less dead; nor that the 'early' death is any less of an outrage upon human feeling. He simply puts all those components of feeling together: 'And her soule ... early ... into heaven (there's a pause until the right word presents itself) ... ravishèd.' Nor does 'the Christian hope' make any difference to the firm past tense of the opening: Ann Donne is 'she whome I *lovd*'. Yet, although he has no possible further claim upon her (the last debt, not only to Nature, but 'to hers' has been paid, stupefyingly paid), that makes no difference to the 'thirst' for more love. How should it? The heart is not appeased by the most impeccable proof that it has no rights. It is inevitable that things should be like that. The 'thirst' is as much a fact as its satisfaction. And if his mind is now wholly set in heavenly things, that is not perhaps the happy state of affairs it might sound: there is a reason – '*Since* she whome I lovd, hath payd her last debt ... and *my good is dead* ... my mind is sett.' The 'since', anyway, might be merely temporal – 'that is what has happened to me since she died. Perhaps it is a good thing. I don't know. But there is no particular merit in it. My good is dead. That is the cost, the source of my dedication.'

You might expect some resentment, some chagrin at least. You would be wrong – or if there is any, it is of an amazingly impersonal kind. The comprehensiveness of the desolation doesn't for one moment negate the reality of wonder which can focus as much upon God as upon her:

> Here the *admyring* her my mind did whett
> To seeke thee God; so streames do shew the head.

I don't pretend to 'understand' the mind that is at work here. To an extent, it's a mind which has moved so far beyond human foible and fretfulness that its calm seems faintly inhuman. And yet, if it is inhuman, it is also deeply natural and it is at pains to honour the natural in human feeling. Implicit in the tone, and in the slow, wondering, halting and haunting movement, one hears an inner voice saying, 'I do not wholly know what this reality is into which I am gazing. It is of the highest importance that I know it as fully as I can; but even more important that I know where my knowledge necessarily leaves off.'

The Sonnet's ending is, as I read it, a 'leaving off' of this kind. The reflections are not strictly relevant, and the 'shape' of the poem, in the sense of its conscious orientation toward meaning, suffers from the irrelevance. And yet the shapeliness of the feeling, the turning aside from what cannot any longer be profitably confronted, is real enough to supply the deficiency. The sad, slow music of the ending, which allows, with some mournful self-knowledge, an inevitable reality to 'the World, fleshe, yea Devill', dies away. The equanimity is not insentience. Nor is it an 'evennesse' plagued with backward glances towards lost pleasures. It is hard-won, hard-held, and it contains real forces. It recognises the very personal route by which Donne has reached faith, and the painful incompleteness of that faith; and it holds to that faith because it is held by it. Divinity, love and wonder are momentarily one.

The Religion of the Natural Man – *Hymnes*

If – as I believe he is – Donne is as much a classic of religious poetry as of love poetry, one would not expect to find the two bodies of 'classicity' existing in hermetic isolation from each other. A classic statement is not specialised in that way. Nor would the connexion merely be a matter of a few 'bridge' poems, half love, half religious lyrics, like 'A Nocturnall' or 'Since she whome I lovd'. It would be a matter of the same fundamental seriousness being able to exercise itself equally, and without specialisation of feeling, in both fields.

When we place the three *Hymnes* against the great love poems, that, I think, is the relationship we see. Both bodies of poetry use the voice of the whole man and draw upon his experience as a whole man. And if they have different 'subjects', the only proper explanation seems to be that something has veritably happened – and happened to the whole man – to change the world he inhabits.

'The whole man' is a precious extract, though, which has to be won out of some fairly amorphous material. We saw the process in the *Songs and Sonets*, as Donne struggled with a congenital irony which was always setting off chain-reactions, converting self-consciousness into self-parody, serious irony into ironic evasiveness. Yet, in a handful of masterpieces, the bonds of that constraining irony were snapped and Donne stepped forth into a new freedom and candour. This newly created self could look back on the self whose currency of feeling and thought had had to be dejectedly coined out of the scrap-metal of love-cliché and it could, as it were, shed its quotation-marks, utter without benefit of *persona*. It could use the simple words of affection and emotion as if they were utterly new:

> Sweetest love, I doe not goe,
> For wearinesse of thee...

> And now good morrow to our waking soules...

Let us love nobly, and live...

So let us melt, and make no noise...

Of course the ironic disciplines had had a great deal to do with the new-minting of this currency; so had the self-explorations by way of role. But role-playing had given way to the one great role of being, and utterance became utterance from that centre.

Something of the same relationship between struggle and achievement holds between the *Holy Sonnets* of the first decade of the seventeenth century and the *Hymnes* of the third decade. Donne's seriousness, in the Sonnets, was still acting itself, showing its paces, trying on roles; and in the effort to be also 'in earnest' it became overblown, operatic. (I take one of the best of the Sonnets so that the comparative judgment won't depend on selective evidence.)

> What if this present were the worlds last night?
> Marke in my heart, O Soule, where thou dost dwell,
> The picture of Christ crucified, and tell
> Whether that countenance can thee affright,
> Teares in his eyes quench the amasing light,
> Blood fills his frownes, which from his pierc'd head fell.
> And can that tongue adjudge thee unto hell,
> Which pray'd forgivenesse for his foes fierce spight?
> No, no; but as in my idolatrie
> I said to all my profane mistresses,
> Beauty, of pitty, foulnesse onely is
> A signe of rigour: so I say to thee,
> To wicked spirits are horrid shapes assign'd,
> This beauteous forme assures a pitious minde.
>
> ('Sonnet 13')

One loses the hypothetical, 'what if' feeling fairly quickly, and the rigid prescriptions of a stereotype devotion ('Marke ... The picture of Christ crucified') are absorbed into a movement of emotion which is genuinely and stormily distraught. But it is still the raised, insistent voice of 'Batter my heart', raised to insist partly because it suspects its own reality. The religiousness in which the Sonnet deals has not yet become native to Donne, and so he cannot find any natural voice to speak of it. The effort is to be as concrete, as actual, as 'present' as possible; but the effort only provides indirect evidence that the actuality has not been achieved and cannot, therefore, be rested in.

At the opposite pole stands the 'Hymne to God the Father':

> I have a sinn of feare that when I have spunn
> My last thred, I shall perish on the shore;
> Sweare by thy self that at my Death, thy Sunn
> Shall shine as it shines nowe, and heretofore;
> And having done that, thou hast done,
> I have noe more.[1]

That is the state, and the progression of feeling which the Sonnet was trying by will and rhetoric to generate – but here it is created, actualised. It is still a religious emotion, of course, radically religious; but a religion that entails no specialisation of feeling, rather a deepening and a broadening of it. Perhaps I can enforce this judgment by adducing Keats's more secular, and yet finally more narrow, handling of the same 'sinn of feare':

> When I have fears that I may cease to be
>   Before my pen has glean'd my teeming brain,
> Before high-piled books, in charactery,
>   Hold like rich garners the full ripen'd grain;
> When I behold, upon the night's starr'd face,
>   Huge cloudy symbols of a high romance,
> And think that I may never live to trace
>   Their shadows, with the magic hand of chance;
> And when I feel, fair creature of an hour,
>   That I shall never look upon thee more,
> Never have relish in the faery power
>   Of unreflecting love; – then on the shore
> Of the wide world I stand alone, and think
> Till love and fame to nothingness do sink.

It's not a negligible poem. But beside the faint note of Keatsian whimpering ('on the shore/Of the wide world I stand alone') and the tendency to die away in a whisper ('Till love and fame to nothingness do sink'), the austerity of temper in the 'Hymne' is the more impressive. Donne is, in a sense, much more radically 'alone' than Keats: his night has no 'starr'd face' or 'Huge cloudy symbols of a high romance', only the long grey line of 'the shore' where he may perish. But he

---

[1] I accept Helen Gardner's arguments for believing that the poem Grierson prints as 'To Christ' is the real and original 'Hymn to God the Father'.

says nothing about his solitude, being too much occupied elsewhere. He may be in the grip of momentous emotion, but if so he will tell us nothing of it: it is reined in to an almost complete monotone – 'Sweare by thy self that at my Death, thy Sunn/Shall shine as it shines nowe, and heretofore' – very little grace of feeling about that, but rather an imperious abruptness. Too much is at stake for Donne to stand on ceremony. Beside that grim monotone, the 'expressive' in Keats's movement and intonation seems slovenly and slack. Donne's voice is 'inexpressive' because of the forces it barely succeeds in containing.

So far I've been talking in terms of 'feare'. Yet this is the Hymne of which Walton's account remains an influential one: 'this heavenly *Hymn*, expressing the great joy that then possest his soul in the Assurance of Gods favour to him when he composed it'. One can only speculate where Walton would have located the 'great joy' in the poem. There is a penitential movement and it does achieve a kind of resolution, but it is a great and *terrible* joy, if joy it is. Because, behind the penitential progression there lies a contrary impulse to evade and defy God:

> Wilt thou forgive that sinn, where I begunn,
>   Which is my sinn, though it were done before?
> Wilt thou forgive those sinns through which I runn
>   And doe them still, though still I doe deplore?
>   When thou hast done, thou hast not done,
>   for I have more.
>
> Wilt thou forgive that sinn, by which I'have wonne
>   Others to sinn, and made my sinn their dore?
> Wilt thou forgive that sinn which I did shunne
>   A yeare or twoe, but wallowed in a score?
>   When thou hast done, thou hast not done,
>   for I have more.

There's a terrible, stealthy joy about the punning declaration that the divine mercy has yet to 'have Donne'. He seems to feel both exultance and desperation at the fact that he 'has more'. It is not, as a twentieth-century scepticism would have it, love subverted by a deeper terror, nor, as Walton wants it, terror sweetly dispelled by love, but the religious emotion born of both, a unique compound of feeling which any careful reader of the great religious classics should be familiar with:

Wert thou mine enemy, O thou my friend,
How wouldst thou worse, I wonder, than thou dost
Defeat, thwart me?
                (Hopkins, 'Thou art indeed just, Lord')

Only by way of recognising that paradoxical religious awe can we interpret the abruptness with which Donne calls for 'Assurance of Gods favour', demanding with blasphemous impertinence the oath 'by thy self' which was Jehovah's oath to Abraham and his seed. And only this way does the ambiguity of the last line – 'I have no more' – become intelligible and operative. It is the end of his fears, one would have thought, and the beginning of his pardon. There are no more concealed sins. And yet the note of exhaustion is unmistakable, exhaustion bordering on insensibility. When God 'has Donne' it is partly because Donne himself – emptied, evacuated of all feeling, a man who has 'no more' – has neither resource nor motive for further resistance. The 'feare' of the last stanza, notice, has not been fear of hell, but of extinction, a pagan 'perishing on the shore', never even setting out on the great voyage of eternity. One possibility the ending envisages is that the mercy of God is simply another version of the same personal extinction. Against that assailing fear Donne pushes up into the breach all the sin he can discover in himself – sins of increasing seriousness, that may postpone the appalling hiatus when God has done, and his destiny falls upon him.

Fear is only half the poem, though, and it would be a lesser thing if it were all. The 'sonne' and 'Sunn' do shine, and have done 'heretofore'. That is not in question. The sin is not merely paganly clung to; it is also religiously abhorred. The degradation he feels, in making the confessions he must make, in gradually ripping up the protective coverings that have skinned the vice on the top, is palpable – 'And doe them *still*, though *still* I doe deplore'.

However, degraded though he is, Donne never topples over into the indulgence of self-disgust. He knows his own nature too well to be shocked at this late date. The tone is one of grimly humorous understatement through a set jaw:

Which is *my* sinn, *though* it were done before.

The wrigglings of self-excuse, sardonically anticipated, are as mercilessly trodden out. Donne manages thus to be utterly rigorous, without losing that last grain of good-humoured self-possession. It's a crucial reservation: the good humour is what prevents self-arraignment ending in moral bankruptcy, with the self shattered and broken by its own excessive rigours.

But couldn't it also be argued that the good-humour reveals the same vestigial attachment to the unregenerate self which – it was my case – disrupted the conscious aims of the *Holy Sonnets*? The answer is, No, and the reason is that the 'conscious aims' of the 'Hymne' have been tempered by being plunged into the well of unconscious feelings and desires. The deep irresolution is recognised and accepted. Donne certainly wants to be rid of the slippery ironist in himself, the one who can never be pinned down. But he has also lived long enough with himself to have developed a rough affection for his *alter ego*. That, I think, is the most powerful effect of the central pun on his name: the theological consequences of being like this may be appalling, but that is the man Donne knows himself to be, and there is no changing it – not even if you are God:

> When thou hast done, thou hast not done,
> for I have more.

What necessarily escapes my 'explanation' of this marvellously creative and intelligent word-play, of course, is the simultaneity of meaning. The sane worldliness which is at home with the insurrection against God is identical with a dangerous defiance which imperils the soul. The comic and the tragic views of the case are co-extensive and indivisible, and Donne makes his peace with them both by means of a wit that is as calmly acquiescent as it is deeply troubled.

The 'Hymne to God my God, in my sicknesse' takes a different view of the troubled waters in which Donne finds himself:

> I joy, that in these straits, I see my West;
> For, though theire currants yeeld returne to none,
> What shall my West hurt me?

'I joy ...' – truly astonishing, if truly felt. This is incomparably the most serenely affirmative of the *Divine Poems* – so much so that the serenity would be outrageous, if there were the least suspicion of its being consciously worn, or flaunted. One of the more disgusting manifestation of piety is a parade of supernal calm in the face of the last issues, when everyone is well aware that the last issues are comfortably far off. It's a cheap forgery, for moral effect, of a courage which is rare and irreplaceable. The 'Hymne' depends for its power upon convincing the reader that it is indeed death that is being confronted, and no homiletic simulacrum of it.

Yet Donne has denied himself the most obvious resource – there is no shouted drama of terror to impress the reality upon us ('Oh my blacke Soule! now art thou summoned'). It is not to be that kind of departure. When virtuous men pass mildly away, they 'whisper to their soules, to goe'. Donne is here, you might say, whispering to his soul. Yet even that is to imply drama, though of a different kind, and the note is plainer still; the voice-level is that of everyday, household conversation.

Actually, a house is exactly where the conversation does seem to be taking place – a house somewhat disrupted by sickness, with one room given over to the patient and his physicians, but a house nonetheless. The air of drama in that room is in such contrast to the domestic ordinariness of the rest that it appears to amuse Donne as he lies helplessly at the mercy of his helpers:

> Whilst my Physitians by their love are growne
> Cosmographers, and I their Mapp, who lie
> Flat on this bed...

It's as if, with that odd sensation of detachment from one's own body that sometimes comes with illness, he were catching a glimpse, through the doorway, of the medical deliberations over his prostrate self and comically misconstruing the scene.

The other 'roome' we hear of is, startlingly enough, the antechamber of heaven. But if this is not, as it appears, the same 'Holy roome' as the one where Donne already lies, it is the next room, and nothing but a half-opened door separates him from it.

> Since I am comming to that Holy roome,
> Where, with thy Quire of Saints for evermore,
> I shall be made thy Musique; As I come
> I tune the Instrument here at the dore,
> And what I must doe then, thinke now before.[1]

[1] I accept Helen Gardner's emendation of this line. Grierson's 'thinke *here* before' has no MS. authority and it destroys the then/now antithesis.

Even the preparation for death, the practice of the Christian *ars mori-endi*, which tended for Donne's contemporaries (and for Donne himself, at his death) to be an occasion of gorgeous theatricality, is kept on the domestic scale. One must, of course, prepare, not arrive all slubbered and slovenly at the gates of death. It's a matter of simple politeness for a musician not to irritate his audience with sawings and screwing; he does that, naturally, at the door, where he may be heard, but will not annoy. It's nothing but the plainest good sense to think now what one must do then. But the 'Musique' is what matters.

This 'tuning' of the affections, to which the rest of the poem is devoted, this fixing of exactly the right pitch, is what makes possible the poetry's own music. Without it, the 'Hymne' is merely ingenious, its elaborate deployment of analogy no more than ornate, and its subtle knitting of the argument into a conclusion merely a doctrinal point clinched. But because the pitch is absolutely true, all these devices become subject to the harmony of the emotion. No single word will describe it: neither diffident nor ostentatious, neither ignoble nor elevated, neither humbly domestic nor consciously grand. All one can say is that it is an utterance by which the high seriousness is human-ised, and the household usualness given a unique dignity.

Music is the consummate manifestation of balance, of tension skil-fully tempered – sometimes painfully (if one is, like Donne, the instrument), but always in measure. And 'thy Musique' is the master-image, in this poem, for the supreme human beatitude: no higher destiny is envisaged for man, than to be 'made thy Musique'. It's a faith, of course, that can never be validated, or demonstrated. It can only be shown to be consonant with the states which precede and lead up to it – consonant with such feelings as

I joy, that in these straits, I see my West.

Again the pun becomes the creative instrument of an ambiguity in experience which cannot be resolved: in such deathly extremity (in these straits) Donne may well 'joy' to see the end approaching, and a bitter joy it is; but equally the 'straits' mark, and he sees 'in' them, the great and joyous turning point in the greatest of all voyages. Each perception tempers the other. So, too, the fearful heat (*fretum*) of the fever may be simultaneously the strait (*fretum*) which leads out of these vexed waters. And the frightening undertow of currents which 'yeeld returne to none' may be seen as leading only to 'my West', a calm and glowing end to a perilous day. Given that utter composure of feeling, which has nevertheless seen all that might terrify, given this warmly humane result of thinking now before what must be done then, and given the poem itself as Donne's way of 'tuning the Instrument here at the dore', it is possible also to be haunted by the echo of that impossible celestial 'Musique' for which it is a preparation.

It's perhaps worth remarking that Donne has grounded his conviction of the double aspect of death on another of the great primal metaphors – the waters of death. (Isn't it the mark, incidentally, of the truly great writer that when he meets the big cruxes his instinct is always to reach for the things that have always been thought true?) River Jordan is deep and wide, whether it's being crossed by a blues singer, or by the Hebrew poet ('I sink in deep waters; the billows go over my head; all the waves go over me'), or by Bunyan's Christian who quotes him. Donne's strait differs only in running with a current so powerful that one cannot even 'go over', only permit oneself to be carried by it to unknowable destinations.

But on the same waters (isn't it possible?) we may sail to 'discoverie'. And the word begins to fill with amazing meaning. After the fearful turbulence of the straits, if only we allow ourselves to be carried, we may pass into unforeseeable calm – the pacific sea, broad, spacious, unmarked by human passage. Our world, yet unearthly: the utterly pristine and new. What shall my West hurt me, if it is like that? By identifying dissolution and discovery as taking place on the same 'sea', Donne appeals to our sense that the experience of being caught in those icy currents of the end contains *both* feelings.

We're only halfway through the poem, and I don't want to go on pedantically expounding the argument. It would only falsify it anyway. Donne left the logical gaps between his analogies, and the emotional gaps between the stanzas, because his mind was moving with exhilarated freedom between regions of experience whose connexion could only clumsily be spelt out. It looks like a theology we're being offered and it is; but it proceeds from that state of mute and marvelling attentiveness when things simply present themselves to the mind, and the mind records them:

> We thinke that *Paradise* and *Calvarie*,
> > *Christs* Crosse, and *Adams* tree, stood in one place;

Looke Lord, and finde both *Adams* met in me;
As the first *Adams* sweat surrounds my face,
May the last *Adams* blood my soule embrace.

At the moment of most explicitly theological speculation, Donne's awareness of his physical state as a sick man is at its sharpest – tactilely you might almost say, looking at that sweat-*surrounded* face (because sweat does in fact pour most profusely from the hair and run *round* the face). The theology is there, not as an explanation of what is happening to the sick man, but because it is as much a part of what he feels as the sweat is.

And yet ... the 'theological' in the poem is what one has perhaps most cause to hesitate over; certainly it's what the modern reader finds hardest to come to terms with. In a sense it is a theological affirmation on which the whole argument pivots –

So death doth touch the Resurrection –

and on which it ends –

Therfore that he may raise the Lord throws down.

I think I've said enough to show that this can't be the *conclusion* of a poem which is so magnificently an experience not a theory; but the relation between experience and theory remains a puzzling one. It's not something, finally, that admits of explanation, but a comparison may help to define the special way in which the theology is present in the 'Hymne'. It is Herbert's poem 'Death'.

Death, thou wast once an uncouth hideous thing,
Nothing but bones,
The sad effect of sadder grones:
Thy mouth was open, but thou couldst not sing.

For we consider'd thee as at some six
Or ten yeares hence,
After the losse of life and sense,
Flesh being turn'd to dust, and bones to sticks.

We lookt on this side of thee, shooting short;
Where we did finde
The shells of fledge souls left behinde,
Dry dust, which sheds no tears, but may extort.

148

> But since our Saviours death did put some bloud
> Into thy face;
> Thou art grown fair and full of grace,
> Much in request, much sought for as a good.
> For we do now behold thee gay and glad,
> As at dooms-day;
> When souls shall wear their new aray,
> And all thy bones with beautie shall be clad.
> Therefore we can go die as sleep, and trust
> Half that we have
> Unto an honest faithfull grave;
> Making our pillows either down, or dust.

The immediate point of comparison with the 'Hymne' lies in the unflustered calm, the homeliness of Herbert's manner, his refusal to be stampeded into panic excess, and his determination to place what terror he admits death to possess in as plainly sensible a context as possible. It is a kindly and dignified poem. But there is also about it – and you will search the 'Hymne' in vain for anything like it – an element of play – rather more attractively good-natured than Donne's comparable 'play' in 'Death be not proud', but play nevertheless. Play enters the metaphors ('The shells of fledge souls left behind', 'our Saviours death did put some bloud/Into thy face'), gets into the tone Herbert feels it appropriate to mock Death in ('Nothing but bones'), and imparts, at its most apt, a modest strength of understatement to Herbert's affirmations, as in that 'honest faithfull grave' where the poem reaches its most sombre intensity. In a sense this is also the note of sane, usual, and domestic calm which distinguishes the 'Hymne to God my God'. But the playfulness, when all is said and done, is a limitation. It is the mark of a mind not willing wholly to commit itself to its own absurdities. It 'plays' because it is afraid it might be thought childish and wishes to anticipate the charge. When Herbert proposes to himself a radical transformation, as a result of Christ's death, of the aspect death presents, some feeling that this is absurd, that death is neither 'full of grace' nor 'much in request' (but a feeling he is not prepared to acknowledge) creeps into the verse and makes it rather coy:

> But since our Saviours death did put some bloud
> Into thy face;

Thou art grown fair and full of grace,
Much in request, much sought for as a good.

With Donne it is different: his is an adulthood sufficiently secure to
be unafraid of being thought childish. He does not attempt to ration-
alise the processes of salvation, which can only be made foolish by
being explained; he just states his request in all its monstrous sim-
plicity:

As the first *Adams* sweat surrounds my face,
May the last *Adams* blood my soule embrace.

So, in his purple wrapp'd receive mee Lord,
By these his thornes give me his other Crowne.

The theology is appealed to as if it were *there*; and thus, for the reader,
it is there. This is the very antithesis of self-conscious play. And yet it
goes with the self-awareness which has Donne catch himself up at this
point and, with a beautiful implicit humour, recognise that the
preacher in his nature has got loose again. He has some excuse of
course: he has been a long time preaching to 'others soules'. But that
doesn't mean that his first and final address should not be to himself;
and, recovering the seriousness which has never really been en-
dangered, he *makes* that first and final address, both 'Text' and
'Sermon', on which the poem ends:

And as to others soules I preach'd thy word,
Be this my Text, my Sermon to mine owne,
Therfore that he may raise the Lord throws down.

In the 'Hymne to God my God, in my sicknesse', the amount of
Donne's feeling which flows into the theology of his condition may
make the poem difficult of access now, and perhaps a lesser achieve-
ment than the other two *Hymnes*. I'm not sure. But that the feeling
does *flow*, and is never dammed, diverted, or piped off to drive mental
wheels for the grinding of metaphysical axes – of that I am entirely
sure.

I am equally sure that 'A Hymne to Christ, at the Authors last going
into Germany' (which is where I shall end) is one of the greatest
religious lyrics in the language. Perhaps it's significant that, like 'A
Hymne to God the Father', and unlike the 'Hymne to God my God,
in my sicknesse', it's a poem which preserves the tension between the

fear and the love of God – which tension seems the most abiding feature of Donne's relations with the deity. Though perhaps not. In any case, that's a psychological speculation one leaves very rapidly behind once one starts reading the 'Hymne to Christ'. Such questions were relevant to the more tumultuous of the *Holy Sonnets*, but it would be impertinent (in both senses), faced with this poem, to demand what it is that drives Donne to serve a God who moves him as much to terror as to love. One recognises the moment the question is put that there is an immovable sub-stratum of attachment which has nothing to do with satisfaction or happiness or fulfilment. As Donne insists in the Sermon contemporaneous with this poem (the Valedictory Sermon of 18 April 1619), one chooses a religion 'seeing it to be ... simply good in it self, and not good by reason of advantage, or conveniency, or other collateral and by-respects'.

That thing 'simply good in it self' presents obvious conceptual difficulties. It is scarcely accessible to language at all, language being a matter of relation and comparison between realities, whereas this reality refuses all relation and comparison. But behind the philosophical imperviousness lies a human feeling – the reaching out for some commitment utterly disinterested, unconcerned with reward or punishment, above the mere pursuit of personal happiness. The thing simply good in itself may be finally inaccessible to intelligence and impossible of communication, but the feeling of pursuing it is not. And even the self-authenticating joy of apprehending it can be rendered: Dante, contemplating 'the scattered leaves of all the universe, bound by love in one volume', the paradisal vision of the Divine Unity, beautifully captures the *process* of authentication:

> La forma universal di questo nodo
> credo ch'io vidi, perchè più di largo
> dicendo questo, mi sento ch'io godo.

(The universal form of this complex I believe I beheld, since more largely – or more freely, spaciously – as I say this, I feel myself rejoicing.) He does not rejoice *because* he has seen it – that would be the interested self-exaltation of the spiritual snob. He believes he *has* seen it because he finds that in himself which is already rejoicing, and which quickens as he approaches this region of memory.

What goes for the beatific vision goes also for the renunciation it may motivate: Donne does not renounce the world because he has discovered higher joys – that would be a vulgarly prudential piety, very much tainted with 'advantage' and 'conveniency' – a matter of spiritual reinvestment in richer securities. Rather, in a manner which is madness to the world of 'conveniency', he measures the preciousness of the faith by the costliness of the sacrifices he discovers himself already making for it. It is not a setting of a price upon salvation, followed by a down-payment, so much as the progressive, astonished discovery of the extent of his own unperceived, irrevocable involvement.

Again it's a truth to experience that one can only illustrate by appeal to other great religious classics. 'Ash Wednesday', for instance:

> At the first turning of the third stair
> Was a slotted window bellied like the fig's fruit
> And beyond the hawthorn blossom and a pasture scene
> The broadbacked figure drest in blue and green
> Enchanted the maytime with an antique flute.
> Blown hair is sweet, brown hair over the mouth blown,
> Lilac and brown hair;
> Distraction, music of the flute, stops and steps of
> the mind over the third stair,
> Fading, fading; strength beyond hope and despair
> Climbing the third stair.
>
> Lord, I am not worthy
> Lord, I am not worthy
> but speak the word only.

The process is not even properly 'renunciation'. Not the evacuation of the world of love and life – blown hair is, and remains, sweet; the stops as much as the steps of the mind are a part of its natural rhythm; it is just 'fading, fading'. And as the poet finds in himself the unsuspected impulse and resource to climb, he is also, at the same time, tapping 'strength beyond hope and despair'.

That's the strength, too, of the 'Hymne to Christ'. And like the best things in 'Ash Wednesday' it achieves its power as music by finding in language the perfect formal equivalent for the natural rhythm, 'the stops and steps of the mind' which is climbing this particular stair. I shall not name the stair, since Eliot wouldn't: the naming has a horrible tendency to place it in the category of spiritual exercises – which is what it most precisely is not. Spiritual exercises presume a known self with a known destination. Religious poetry of the kind we're considering is instinct with wonder; wonder at the self and at the infinitude of its possible destinations.

The formal perfection of the 'Hymne to Christ', though, is paramount – and not to be nailed by analysis: we need some subtler instrument of intelligence if we are to touch the poem's quick without destroying it. George Eliot offers some illuminatingly apposite terms here. 'Poetic form', she says,

was not begotten by thinking it out or framing it as a shell which should hold emotional expression, any more than the shell of an animal arises before the living creature; but emotion, by its tendency to repetition, i.e. rhythmic persistence in proportion as diversifying thought is absent...

[as for instance with:

> Lord, I am not worthy
> Lord, I am not worthy
> but speak the word only.]

...creates a form by the recurrence of its elements in adjustment with certain given conditions of sound, language, action, or environment. Just as the beautiful expanding curves of a bivalve shell are not first made for the reception of the unstable inhabitant, but grow and are limited by the simple rhythmic conditions of its growing life.

That essential organic connexion between 'form', 'rhythm' and 'life' provides a context for understanding the 'music' of Donne's poem.

He is setting out on a voyage, from which (we gather from some remarks in the Valedictory Sermon) he had some fears of not returning. He is leaving an England which contains everything he has held dear. He is going on a mission he has not chosen to a country he does not love. It is, in his mind though not in fact, winter – at least *his* winter, for he is nearing fifty. What can be done with that concatenation of ill-omens? What is the mind's natural rhythm in these circumstances?

The mind starts simply with a conscious use of the omens as 'emblemes'. All things are contained in God, the 'torne ship', the 'swallowing' sea, the lowering stormy sky, these are all God. He is not consoling himself; the comparisons work both ways, thus proving themselves already *more* than 'emblemes' – the 'Arke' of the church is a 'torne' vessel and it bears him away from all he loves; Christ's blood is a swallowing gulf. But (and now the poem's emotional movement

begins to gather way) behind the clouds of divine displeasure, he tries
by a plangent earnest pleading to prove, are the undespising eyes of
God. The plea is that God will ratify this faith ... and yet those eyes *do*
'turne away sometimes ...'

> In what torne ship soever I embarke,
> That ship shall be my embleme of thy Arke;
> What sea soever swallow mee, that flood
> Shall be to mee an embleme of thy blood;
> Though thou with clouds of anger do disguise
> Thy face; yet through that maske I know those eyes,
> Which, though they turne away sometimes, they never will
> despise.[1]

Already the urgent intonation betrays the pressure of doubt: 'I *know*
those eyes', 'they *never will* despise'. ('O Lord, you would not do that
to me! I know you ...') There is a fundamental faithlessness in the
insistence. By propounding to himself what God will *not* do to him,
Donne engraves upon his mind an image of dereliction it was already
too apt to entertain. Now it cannot be erased.

As between all the stanzas, because there is an expressive break in
the continuity of sense and feeling, we become aware of the unutterable
silence into which these pleas are falling. There is no response. Perhaps
more is expected of him. He concentrates himself for what now pre-
sents itself as the inevitable next step – lower, descend lower. As the
descent begins the composure only becomes more palpable:

> I sacrifice this Iland unto thee,
> And all whom I lov'd there, *and* who lov'd mee...

(I do not forget that the sacrificing costs pain to those who have least
deserved it, and it is not only my love – which is mine to sacrifice – but
theirs – which is not mine to give – that I am casting aside.)

> ...When I have put our seas...

(theirs *and* mine – the bond of tears and the sea of separation)

> ...twixt them and mee,
> Put thou thy sea betwixt my sinnes and thee...

[1] For some reason, which has never been clear to me, editors break up this concluding
seven-stress line – which Donne very skilfully exploits for its rhythmic fluidity –
into a rigid and jingly ballad metre of four-plus-three. Since the long line is in all
the MSS., the emendation seems gratuitous.

and it's no use looking for the logic of that bargain: it is Donne bargain-
ing in the dark, unable to be sure what is demanded of him, or if
anything is demanded of him. 'Surely', he says, 'since I have nothing
greater than this to give, since this is everything, surely this will
purchase my forgiveness' – though the discrepancy between the
limited physical seas of the Channel and the vaster seas of absolution
through Grace points up the fortuitousness of the entailment. Yet for
a brief moment an inner rightness about this withdrawal upon the self
takes hold of him. It may not be what he wishes, but it is what he
must. The rightness takes him beyond thinking in terms of *emblems*,
to which meaning can only hopefully be assigned, to a metaphor that
asserts a necessary truth, and a natural rhythm:

> As the trees sap doth seeke the root below
> In winter, in my winter now I goe,
> Where none but thee, th'Eternall root of true Love I may know.

This is a point of rest. A harmony which, by its unearthly blend of
tremulousness and joy, its deep solemnity and its sensuous delicacy,
creates a meaning for that 'root of true Love' in a world beyond even
human love, though organically related to it, as root to leaves. And
the 'seeking' movement of the sap is at once involuntary, natural, and
the fulfilment of the deepest kind of *purpose*.

But now the mind turns back on itself, with a *non sequitur* puzzling
at first, but moving as one grasps its intent:

> Nor thou nor thy religion dost controule,
> The amorousnesse of an harmonious Soule...

Does the sacrifice have to be so complete? Isn't there ample room
within the love of heaven for these other loves, the love of natural
things, the 'amorousnesse of an harmonious Soule'?

> But thou would'st have that love thy selfe.

And with a horrible indecorum Donne finds himself urging the sophis-
tries of a very human and dependent love, upon God – as if He were
his mistress. The emotional disarray is complete. He demands the
obliteration of all other love as being God's responsibility. Then he
laments the very liberty given him to do this for himself, claiming it
as a refinement of tyranny, which knows that the granting of liberty

only makes the sense of obligation more overwhelming. And finally, since God will do nothing to settle his allegiances, he turns in humiliation and accusation, claiming that inaction which grants him his liberty, as a proof that 'thou lov'st not mee'.

> As thou
> Art jealous, Lord, so I am jealous now,
> Thou lov'st not, till from loving more, thou free
> My soule: Who ever gives, takes libertie:
> O, if thou car'st not whom I love alas, thou lov'st not mee.

Yet the lines, at the very moment that they dramatise the utter abjection of dependency, are showing the faint growing awareness that it is precisely that refusal to enter upon so unequal a relation, precisely the refusal to exploit Donne's abjection, that constitutes *this* God's deepest claim upon him: whoever takes, in this way, also gives liberty. Again the silence between the stanzas falls. Donne wrestles with the inalienable responsibility for his own fate, of which not even God will relieve him – the necessity that he make his own commitment in full possession of his manhood.

Well, perhaps that is just it; perhaps indeed 'thou lov'st not mee'. You will not free me from these clinging human loves. What then? That is a 'collateral and by-respect'. I do not love because I am loved, but because what I love is 'simply good in it self'. As such, it cannot demand anything of anyone. The ultimate gesture of renunciation and acceptance I must make for myself. Very well (and Donne gathers himself in a last effort of composure and recollection, shaking off the emotional disorder of the previous stanza, steadying his voice. The voice that comes is one of extraordinary power and authority, yet also of extraordinary gentleness.)

> Seale then this bill of my Divorce to All,
> On whom those fainter beames of love did fall;
> Marry those loves, which in youth scattered bee
> On Fame, Wit, Hopes (false mistresses) to thee...

The sense of the full value of what is forgone here is implicit in the lingering stress on 'All', and in the beautiful assonantal cadence of '*Marry* those loves, which in youth *scatterèd* bee'; and at the same time we are given the wondering sense that these 'beames' are indeed 'fainter' ('fading, fading') as the will, or rather the whole prepared consciousness comes with delicacy and firmness to rest on its unconscious centre: '*Marry* those loves...scattered...On Fame, Wit, Hopes...to *thee*.'

One may think one knows what is happening here, and that it is something of the kind usually understood by the word 'renunciation'. If so, one needs to pause and look again. It is something more remarkable.

Not that renunciation is a mean or a negligible act: viewed from one angle it may reveal itself as the last and purest heroism. Conrad wrote:

That a sacrifice must be made, that something has to be given up, is the truth engraved in the innermost recesses of the fair temple built for our edification by the masters of fiction. There is no other secret behind the curtain. All adventure, all love, every success is resumed in the supreme energy of an act of renunciation. It is the uttermost limit of our power; it is the most potent and effective force at our disposal...No man or woman worthy of the name can pretend to anything more, to anything greater...Wherever he stands, at the beginning or the end of things, a man has to sacrifice his gods to his passions or his passions to his gods.[1]

As a critique of the romanticism of false and euphoric finalities, and likewise of the romantic idealism which chooses to burn itself out, gods and all, in a fine blaze of self-destructive passion, that comes with welcome trenchancy. But Conrad's 'gods', postulated here as existing in eternal antagonism to the 'passions', are still, in their very antagonism, romantic deities, and they glow dully with a heat for which renunciation itself might be no more than an alleviation and an indulgence. The 'renunciation' of the 'Hymne' is, by comparison, passionless, bleak, and final. The possibility it figures (and it is figured equally by the 'Nocturnall' and 'Since she whome I lovd') is that, beyond the romantic battleground where passions and gods contend in fierce emulation, there may be some silent ground of naturalness – which it would be folly either to seek out or to shun, but which may, ineluctably, disclose itself as the real. Then, when we have ceased to distinguish the end of things from their beginning; when, at the year's midnight and the day's, in winter, in our winter, our good is dead, and we are

---

1 'Henry James: An Appreciation', *Notes on Life and Letters* (1949), pp. 15–16.

beyond renunciation having nothing left worth renouncing; then we may also find we no longer have to choose between our passions and our gods, because we have been stripped of both.

It may – indeed it does – seem unaccountable to be calling utterance from that state of moral and human destitution, 'great poetry'. I can offer no resolution to that paradox. How, even, it might conceivably come about, that the choice should make itself in a way that requires no sacrifice, cannot be explained – only remarked when it does come about. In the remaining three lines of the 'Hymne', it comes about. A presence enters the poem, in the face of which the calm of mind imperfectly grasped in the earlier lines, becomes a simple immediacy of feeling. The change is signalled first by a near frivolity – except that in so solemn a context one knows it must be something else:

> Churches are best for Prayer, that have least light.

As a reason for choosing 'an Everlasting night' that is shockingly, frivolously insufficient. But then, reasons themselves are collateral and by-respects, and Donne marks his awareness of this by the half-smile of comprehension and acceptance which crosses his face as he moves into the darkness. On another level, anyway, that twilight realm of the darkened church, which is prayer's native element, may answer to some deeper night in the soul which seeks it out. Not a darkness that gives way to day, but 'an Everlasting night'.

This is what Donne chooses – or perhaps recognises himself to have already chosen; in either case, the choice is now affirmed in full knowledge. He chooses it in order merely (and it would be absurd if it were the real reason – but there is no reason) 'to scape stormy days'. And he goes out, the bride of darkness, with something one is astonished to feel as a kind of gladness; but a very strange kind which is neither black nihilism and despair, nor exultation and joy – but that *tertium quid*, neither and both, the religious emotion, awe carried to the supreme pitch which is darkness, stillness, nothingness. It is one of the rare moments in literature when one has some idea of what it might mean to 'behold God', confront the absolutely other, the non-, the anti-human, which is also supremely, and humanly, desired.

> Churches are best for Prayer, that have least light:
> To see God only, I goe out of sight:
> And to scape stormy dayes, I chuse an Everlasting night.

'The simple rhythmic conditions of the growing life' are fulfilled. The shell is complete. The poem ends.

If it is the function of a poet, not only to discover new expressive resources for meeting new ways of feeling, but also (quickened by that newness into some keener intuition of continuities) to reanimate in the present the great words of past experiencings, then Donne has performed this function largely for the language of religion. Words like 'Love', or 'Sinne', or 'God', he has restored to their living context, rooted them in nature, and attuned them to the natural breathing rhythms of a religion of wonder. It is in every way a classic achievement, and one which makes nonsense finally of distinctions between the secular and the religious. There is no fissure into which the wedge might be insinuated. Equally in the great love lyrics and the great religious poems, there is a spaciously conceived human nature, for the 'delight, honour, and benefit' of which this poetry has done, and goes on doing, a great deal; and there is the intimation – which comes upon us with 'that comprehension and expanse of thought which at once fills the whole mind' – of vaster spaces where the act of perception becomes also a participation in vision. Beyond, or behind that, one does not look. The poetry is complete and fulfilled. It inhabits a world of feeling which is natural, just, and – can it not now be granted? – true.

That at least is the kind of reply I should wish to make to Dr Johnson, and the way I should choose to expand Dr Leavis's 'inevitable rightness'. This Donne (if I have not invented him) is a classic who need fear nothing from the vagaries of critical fashion, the apostasy of his prophets – or even from the industry of his expositors.

Index of Poems Discussed